ATLANTIC CITY

DIARY

A CENTURY OF MEMORIES
1880 — 1985

By Ed Davis

ATLANTIC CITY DIARY

Copyright © 1980
by
Ed Davis

Published by
Atlantic Sunrise Publishing Company, McKee City, NJ
in cooperation with
THE SIRACUSA REAL ESTATE & INSURANCE COMPANY,
ATLANTIC CITY

Library of Congress Catalog Card No. 80-53804

ISBN: 0-9614585-1-8
ISBN: 9614585-2-6 (Hardcover)
First Printing: November 1980
Second Printing: May 1981

Second Edition: March 1986

Printed in the United States of America
by BookMasters, Ashland, Ohio

This book is lovingly dedicated
to my wife, Helen
in appreciation of her interest, guidance and suggestions
in its preparation, and her patience during the
countless hours I spent at the typewriter, away from her.

PREFACE

Believe it or not, Atlantic City is on an Island, Absecon Island, aptly described as "The island you can drive to." Absecon Island, named for the Absegami Indians, annually plays host to millions of visitors from all over the world. These people are attracted to our City by many things, some don't cost a cent. Our weather is conducive to much outdoor activity year around. This includes bicycling on the famous Boardwalk, strolling on the white sandy beaches which parallel the Boardwalk, and just plain strolling along the wooden way, stretching eight miles from the Inlet to Ventnor.

Founded in 1854, Atlantic City was at one time, a tiny fishing village. It received its real life's blood with the coming of the railroads. Even today, fishing, both commercial and sport, is a major attraction luring thousands annually to the ocean and bays.

Atlantic City boasts some of the largest conventions. They return year after year, to our huge Convention Hall, and our modern hotels and motels. Night life in our town is something which has gained a reputation for variety over the years, and with the arrival of the Casino era, the stars are bigger and better than ever.

Early in its career, Atlantic City realized its potential as a spot for having fun and its theatres and piers always featured stellar entertainment in one form or another. This included stars of the music world, the sports scene, and the dramatic stage. During the heyday of the big bands, the Marine Ballroom on Steel Pier, and the Ballroom of the States on the Million Dollar Pier featured just about every famous orchestra. People packed in, many to dance, and a large number merely to stand and watch. Glenn Miller, Benny Goodman, Artie Shaw, Jean Goldkette, Paul Whiteman, Charlie Barnet, The Dorseys, Gene Krupa, Harry James, Stan Kenton, and Rudy Vallee were signed to return year after successful year. Some of our big hotels featured name entertainment and the clubs had their share of big names, with the 500 Club, the Paradise, the Club Harlem, Lamb's Club, and Babette's vying for the stars.

It looked like it would never end, but it did. Atlantic City's demise was a slow process, scarcely noticeable to those of us who lived or worked here every day. But it was happening, and before we knew it, people weren't coming to see us much anymore, and those who did stayed for only a day or two, and often unhappily, saying we didn't have anything to offer the visitor anymore. So, they looked for greener pastures, and the Airlines helped, by providing attractive fares to places like Las Vegas and Miami Beach.

The City's hotels and motels deteriorated and it looked like all was lost. The problem was discussed day after day, but it was not until Casino Gaming entered into the talks that a unified effort was made. The rest is current history. Casino Gaming became a reality for Atlantic City, and now it is well on the way to resuming its international position as the Queen of Resorts.

As this is being written we have three Hotel Casinos in operation: Resorts International, Caesars Boardwalk Regency, and Bally's Park

Place, and this is only the beginning. It is predicted that before the end of this decade we will have at least twenty new Hotel Casino establishments. Stars of stage, screen, and television are the entertainment fare nowadays, and the various hotels are competing for the top names.

This book was compiled to provide a look at some of the things that have happened in and to our town, over the century. We couldn't have hoped to capture it all between the covers of one volume. It's a sampling of the atmosphere of our good old days, and yes, our bad old days, too. The exciting and the thrilling . . . the beautiful and the bizarre. They all had their place in the history of our town, a town I first visited as a boy in 1930. I returned every year and in 1946, got a job at radio station WFPG. Many of you reading this go back a lot farther than I, and will recall, first hand, some of the happenings I only heard about or learned through the pages of old books and newspapers. If it helps you to recall a forgotten song, or an event which was shrouded in the mists of time, or has brought back for a moment or two, happier times, then it has accomplished its purpose. I am grateful to the many people who helped make this book possible. They are too numerous to mention here, but they know of my appreciation.

Ed Davis
Atlantic City

THE SIRACUSA STORY

Antonio S. Siracusa

The story of the City of Atlantic City would not be complete if it failed to tell about the Siracusa family. This devoted family has a distinguished record of faithful, dedicated service to the community for the past 90 years - a dedication that has been handed down from father to son for nine decades. It is an inspiring saga spanning four generations.

It all began in 1888 when young Antonio S. Siracusa arrived in the United States to represent his father, a lemon merchant in Sicily. Antonio was fascinated with America, and Atlantic City in particular. He decided to settle here, where he married Lucy Ruffu in 1890. An astute, personable gentleman, Antonio founded the real estate and insurance company bearing the family name. He remained as its head from 1894 until his death in 1919.

A practical visionary, Antonio Siracusa demonstrated his confidence in the future of his beloved City when he built one of its first brick hotels at 121 South Mississippi Avenue, opposite what later became the site of the Convention Hall. It opened as the Siracusa Hotel in 1903, and consisted of 110 rooms. It is standing to this day. He was one of the largest developers of small homes and boarding houses in the 4th Ward. He also built three theaters: the Central, later called the Lyric, the Liberty, later named the Astor, and the Anita Theater on the Boardwalk at Florida Avenue.

John R. Siracusa, Sr., the second generation of the family to work in the company was serving with the U.S. Army in France during World War I when he was notified of his father's demise on February 1, 1919. He received an honorable discharge and returned home to join his younger brother Frank in the business. They worked together until 1955 when John bought out Frank's interest. In 1923, at age 26, he became a director of the Guarantee Trust Company, now known as the Guarantee Bank. He served as President of the Atlantic City Real Estate Board in 1926 and 1927. In 1962, John, Sr. went into semi-retirement, but still continues to be active as advisor and consultant in the business.

Now, John R. Siracusa, Jr., as President of Siracusa Company, has been carrying on the family tradition of service. He joined the Siracusa Company firm in 1950 after serving with the U.S. Marine Corp. during World War II. He is a past president of the Atlantic City Chamber of Commerce, a former Atlantic County Freeholder, and is currently a Board Member of the Atlantic City Medical Center and Guarantee Bank.

A fourth generation Siracusa, J. Eugene, joined the firm in 1974, and is now Vice-President of Siracusa Company. Recently James, another son, has entered the fold. They have the distinction, a unique one, of being the oldest Atlantic City real estate and insurance organization still being operated by the family of its founder.

John, Sr. is looking forward to celebrating his 84th birthday at his desk on August 3, 1980. He has been through the good times and the bad - the roaring 20's, the depression, the war years. He has worked untiringly to help this City when it was at the depths of depression, but he never lost faith in its return as Queen of Resorts. He recalls the sad period when fortunes were lost overnight in Atlantic City. He points with pride to the fact that his uncle, Anthony M. Ruffu, was Mayor of Atlantic City during the 1927-30 era of boom and bust. John, Sr. tells of yet another Siracusa, his brother Anthony J., who served as City Solicitor and as Atlantic County Assemblyman where he rose to the position of Speaker of the Assembly.

So come what may, the Siracusa family is ever mindful of its heritage and its responsibility to the community. The sponsorship of this book is another indication of the love the Siracusa family has for this great resort.

Sidney Ascher
August 1, 1980

Left to right: John Jr., Eugene, the late John Sr., and James Siracusa.

Atlantic City's First Hotel, no identification. Photo from Mrs. M.A. Fracchione, recopy from the collection of H. Gerald MacDonald.

TABLE OF CONTENTS

1880

The coming of the railroad in the 1850's brought Atlantic City a lot nearer for hundreds of thousands of visitors, and a new rail link between Philadelphia and our town was formally opened on Wednesday, June 16, 1880. Officials of the line made an inaugural run over the route, accompanied by invited guests and members of the press from New Jersey and Philadelphia. It was the newest operation of the West Jersey and Atlantic Railroad Company. A special train of four elegant new cars, with plush upholstery and beautiful appointments made the trip to the shore most enjoyable for the group of notables.

The time of departure was several hours later than had been announced, because of the Cape May Express running off the track and blocking it about a dozen miles below Camden. It so happened that Frank Thompson, General Manager of the Pennsylvania Railroad, was at the scene shortly after the accident occurred, and through his energetic efforts, the track was quickly cleared.

After leaving Camden, only two stops were made: in Wenonah and Newfield. Then it was on to Atlantic City to meet the throng waiting to welcome what proved to be a real boost to Atlantic City's economy . . . the coming of a new railroad in the year 1880.

Following the train's arrival here, a number of speeches were made before the waiting crowd. Elected to manage the affairs of the new venture were George Wood, Israel S. Adams, George Potts, Samuel Lewis, Colonel A. L. Snowden, Charles P. Stratton and others, mostly from the Camden-Philadelphia area. Our Mayor then was Willard Wright.

The population of our town at that time was 5,477.

1881

It took the founders of the First National Bank of Atlantic City only two months to open. A group of foresighted businessmen sat down on March 18, 1881, following a period during which they had canvassed the community, to learn if there was a need for such an institution. The consensus indicated the public would patronize a bank, so it was decided to establish one. Robert D. Kent was its first cashier. It opened for business in a room of the Currie Building near the corner of South Carolina Avenue and Atlantic, on May 23.

The bank later moved to the Bartlett Bank Building, constructed expressly for that purpose. Charles Evans was its first president. There were no dividends that first year, but semi-annual 3 percent dividends were paid later. Invested capital was $50,000. Today, the headquarters of Siracusa Real Estate and Insurance Company are in that building at North Carolina and Atlantic Avenues.

"Lucy", the Margate elephant has been a major attraction downbeach since she was built by a real estate promoter in 1881. She has been standing on the beach, although not at the same location, gazing through sightless eyes at the ocean for almost 100 years. Two similar structures built at about the same time are long gone. One was in Cape

Atlantic Avenue looking North, Bartlett Building in foreground, Atlantic City, N. J.

Pub. by Post Card Dist. Co., Atlantic City, N. J.

May, the other at Coney Island, New York. The huge pachyderm, built of wood and tin, was the brain-child of James V. Lafferty. "Lucy" is some 86 feet long and 65 feet high! Cost of construction was $38,000.

Geo. A. McKeague Co., Copyright 1910.

In 1970, "Lucy" was moved to her present location at Decatur Avenue, Margate, but that's another story covered later, under that year. In her heyday, that elephant was a favorite gathering place for residents and visitors, who enjoyed many a good time at the dances held in the "Turkish Pavillion", adjacent to the old landmark.

The Episcopal Church of the Ascension was incorporated January 3. Services had been held early the previous year under the direction of the Reverend J. Rice Taylor, the church's first rector. The Delaware and Atlantic Telephone Company put in a switchboard that year, with a subscriber list of only ten families. It was located in the tower of the old city hall at Tennessee and Atlantic Avenues.

City officials in '81 included Harry Slape, Mayor; Henry Albertson, City Clerk; James Hitchens, Recorder; James Stokes, Alderman; and Chalkley Leeds, Treasurer.

1882

The Atlantic City Water Works Company gave our town its first "running water" in June of 1882, when it brought artesian well water to the island from the mainland, by means of large pipes stretched across the meadows. Prior to this, we got our water from shallow wells, but salt often caused problems. The first recorded use of electricity here was in July of 1882, when the Atlantic City Gas and Water Company turned on street lights, the first of which was in front of Keuhnle's Hotel, on Atlantic Avenue at South Carolina. It really made a difference compared to the early gas lights.

Colonel George W. Howard, of Washington D. C., was the pioneer pier builder in our city, opening Howard's Pier at the foot of Kentucky Avenue on July 12, 1882. It extended out over the ocean for a length of 650 feet. The pier lasted only one season due to faulty pilings. A September storm destroyed the structure, but its owner was not dismayed and vowed to try again.

The "Daily Union History of Atlantic City and County" reported at the time that the builders of a new and bigger Howard's Pier, to be 200 feet longer than its predecessor, actually "threaded" the ends of heavy logs used as pilings, much as one would thread iron or steel, and tried to screw them into the sand, but alas, the idea proved unsuccessful.

Even then, summer rentals were a dependable source of income for local property owners. Our town then was mainly a summer resort and people flocked here from Philadelphia, New York, Pittsburgh and Washington. Income from such rental could amount to as much as $100 dollars a month, netting a tidy sum over the summer. True, our hotels were very popular but even with rates as low as $6 or $8 per week for some of the nicer ones, many folks preferred the personal homey atmosphere of the "cottages", as they were called, and many sections of the city saw construction of small rooming houses which accommodated perhaps 15 or 20 guests. Some of the older homes, with a large number of bedrooms, were converted to rooming houses, and hosted generations of visitors year after year, as their popularity continued.

1883

The summer of 1883 saw the use of arc lamps at each street end on the boardwalk for the very first time. The previous summer the city had enjoyed electric lighting for street use, but it was not til June 1, 1883, that lines were run down to the boardwalk, and the wooden way took on a new dimension after dark. These lamps were the open arc type. Edison's incandescent lamp still was three years in the future. So, the warm summer nights were enhanced along our promenade, if not for "spooners", who found it too bright, then for those content to stroll and chat. But come September and season's end, the current was cut off! As time went on, individual shops along the 'walk put in the new arc lamps, adding to the brightness.

The Texas Avenue School, with 12 rooms, was erected in 1883, and had a value of $25,000!

Atlantic City has many legends, and one of the most oft-repeated ones concerns the origin of our famous salt water taffy. The story goes that during the summer of '83, a candy merchant, with a boardwalk shop at St. James Place, turned a mishap into a big "plus"! His name was David Bradley, and when a storm tide wet down his stock of taffy candy, Bradley is said to have gotten the bright idea of calling it "salt water" taffy! City directories show no listing of any shops carrying salt water taffy until 1889, so the tale could be merely a pleasant little anecdote, meaning no harm, but attaching a bit of romance to the treat which now is sold in countless other resorts as well. Apparently, the name never was copyrighted and has been used by various candy makers over the years, although the big names in Atlantic City associated with salt water taffy are Fralinger's, James, Phillips and Tripician.

In 1883, our city boasted a number of fine hotels, the largest of which were the United States, taking in a full city block bounded by Atlantic, Delaware, Pacific and Maryland Avenues; Congress Hall, Massachusetts and Congress Avenues; and Surf House, which also took in an entire block, bounded by Atlantic, Kentucky, Pacific and Illinois Avenues. Mayor Charles Maxwell took office that year.

The Children's Seashore House, founded in 1872, was an idea born in Philadelphia, where the majority of its beneficiaries lived. In July, 1883, the institution took possession of a new and commodious building at the ocean end of Ohio Avenue, on the site later occupied by the Marlborough-Blenheim Hotel. Then began extensions and additions of some 14 buildings.

The first construction of homes in what is now known as the Chelsea section of town, began with the organization of the Chelsea Beach Company, a real estate firm, by Mrs. Mary A. Riddle and six other local women, who ventured to develop where no man had previously dared take a chance. The area took in the acreage between what are now Montpelier and Brighton Avenues. Lots on Pacific Avenue were then selling for as little as $500! Steam trains began to run through the property down to Longport at the south end of Absecon Island the following year, further boosting the popularity of the development.

5

1884

By this time, Atlantic City boasted at least three newspapers: "The Atlantic Review" which published "daily and weekly" as their ad stated. Heston and Shreve were the proprietors. The publication was touted as "the leading paper in the city, with the largest circulation in the state, south of Trenton". Another was "The Atlantic Times", with offices at 1630 Atlantic Avenue, which published weekly on Thursdays . . . daily during July and August. J. F. Hall was editor and proprietor.

The "Atlantic Sunday Mail", published by Harold Silberman, editor and owner, at 1214 Atlantic Avenue, advertised that it was "the only Sunday paper in Atlantic City or County". Subscription price was $1.50 per year, making its cost less than 3¢ per copy! These publications probably were for sale at such local newsstands as that at the Seaside Pharmacy, corner Atlantic Avenue and Surf Place, advertised as "a model of neatness, ably conducted by the owner who has had 26 years' experience". It carried "the coldest and most delicious soda water on the island, fine cigars and choice liquors for medicinal use". M. West was the proprietor.

In the winter of 1884, the three-masted schooner, "Robert Morgan", came ashore next to Applegate's Pier during a violent storm on January 9th, landing high and dry with no serious injuries to her crew. The following summer, Atlantic City, even then wise in the ways of promotion, publicized the stranded vessel as a tourist attraction and people came from far and near to view the craft as she lay helpless on the sand.

Photo courtesy Mark J. Collins; Recopy by H.J. Swarts

1885

As noted under the last entry, advertising was quite flowery in the eighties, and local ads were no exception. Mrs. J. C. White's Pioneer Dry

Goods Store, Atlantic below Georgia, featured a full stock of dry goods, and her ad stated that she was "thankful for past favors and a continued patronage is respectfully solicited". Samuel E. Perry practiced law at 1803 Atlantic Avenue, while Slape and Stephany were engaged in the same profession "on Atlantic Avenue opposite the bank building". Today we'd have to ask which bank!

Guvernator's Mammoth Constitution Pavilions and Concert Gardens were advertising to one and all that here was "the resort of the elite of Atlantic City, with a sea view, elegant music, best of refreshments, strict order, grand concerts mornings, afternoons and evenings, electric lights and convenient location, just above the Seaview Excursion House".

The establishment of S. Harkings, 116 Atlantic Avenue near the Mansion House, praised itself as "the cheapest shell store in town with a full line of shells, corals, toys and curiosities". Groceries, coal, glass and "queensware", as well as butter and eggs, were dispensed by C. E. Adams, at 1224 Atlantic Avenue. And Miss M. Duffee, 1322 Atlantic Avenue, was offering a "large stock of ready made waves and ladies' hair dressing in the latest styles, plus a long hair switch for $2.50".

The Atlantic Civil and Criminal Detective Agency was advertising "experienced and reliable detectives for evidence in civil actions, missing persons and absent witnesses. Supervision of waiters in hotels and boarding houses a specialty". How times have changed, when much detail is left to the imagination in modern printed ads.

1886

Over the 126 years of its existence, Atlantic City has had many ocean piers, stretching out over the waves. The first one erected on iron pilings jutted out to sea from the end of Massachusetts Avenue. It was built by the Ocean Pier Company and opened on the 25th of April in 1886. Named "Iron Pier" for obvious reasons, it had a large theatre at the ocean end and for many years featured live stage shows, but the real action was taking place at the center of the boardwalk with its myriad attractions, including exhibits, rides and displays. The public failed to flock to "Iron Pier" as had been hoped by its developers. Twelve years later, it was bought up by the H. J. Heinz Company, the pickle firm in Pittsburgh, Pennsylvania, and underwent extensive alterations. The pier was razed in 1945, following the devastating hurricane of the year before, and we'll be taking a look at the happy times on Heinz Pier later on.

Our boardwalk rolling chairs have an interesting heritage, dating back to 1886 when the city okayed the use of such conveyances for the upcoming year. The first brick house in the resort was built by William J. Moore, in March of '86, at 107 North Tennessee Avenue. Prior to that time, Atlantic City was illuminated by gas lamps along the sidewalks, but the summer of 1886 marked the introduction of electric lighting and folks welcomed the opportunity to stroll under their bright glow.

This same year saw no less than 17 vessels either sunk or damaged off the coast of Absecon Island! Eight of them met disaster in the months of January and February, and the locations of those wrecks were mostly on the Absecon bar. One took place in Little Egg Inlet and one on the hazardous Brigantine Shoals. Old records show that not one life was lost in any of these mishaps!

1887

Merry-go-rounds or carrousels were for years a part of the Atlantic City scene and appealed to the young of all ages! The stationary kind was popular with adults but the ones which moved up and down on a pole were the delight of the younger set! It was a merry-go-round which made John L. Young and Stewart McShea decide to team up in a partnership which resulted in big things happening in the local world of entertainment. In 1887, they purchased the Old Victoria Skating Rink at South Carolina Avenue and the Boardwalk. On the site, they built the Merry-Go-Round Casino and equipped it with the largest carrousel they could find. The establishment featured an orchestrion, a mechanical organ, a collector's item today, which at that time cost $10,000! And they had a record library numbering close to a hundred selections, many of which were sacred music. The building had a roof of glass on the ocean side and was heated in winter. McShea was opposed to Sunday amusements, so on that day only the organ was in operation playing for as many as 3,000 persons sometimes, who sat contentedly in rockers or on benches singing along from hymnals.

A hardware merchant, William Hayday, had rented invalids' wheel chairs for boardwalk use from his shop at 1702 Atlantic Avenue for quite a while, when he saw the potential for another use of the conveyances. Hayday figured that in addition to transporting those unable to walk due to infirmities, the chair on wheels would be just the thing in which to ride for relaxation. So it was that the wicker rolling chair began to gain favor with those who were quite able to walk, but who chose to be

Rolling Chair Comfort, on the Boardwalk, Atlantic City, N. J.

pushed! Little by little, the rolling chairs increased in number and in popularity til their major use was more for pleasure than for transporting the infirm. And a visit to Atlantic City just wasn't complete without a ride in a rolling chair!

Two mayors served the resort during 1887. Thomas C. Garrett and Samuel D. Hoffman.

1888

Most everyone has heard of the famous blizzard of '88, the subject of many oft-told tales, of how hard the wind blew, how high the drifts were and how long it snowed. The storm was widespread, covering almost all of the area from Canada to North Carolina! It began as a light drizzle which increased in intensity til, on Sunday night, March 11th, it changed to snow, accompanied by strong winds and continued throughout the night! On Monday morning, local residents awoke to a world of white with the snow still coming down! It was six feet deep in many places, while in others the ground was almost bare, due to the action of the winds. Old timers tell how it was impossible to see across the street at the height of the storm.

Only a very few of the more hardy ventured out of doors, and those only in cases of dire necessity. Communications with the outside world were virtually cut off! It is recorded as the worst storm of the century, up to that time. The blizzards of 1856 and 1857 had been real bad ones but not nearly so severe as the combination of snow, wind and low temperatures, which wrought havoc along the eastern seaboard, during the historic blizzard of '88!

The first instance of an electric motor being used in Atlantic City was that March, when one of the new contraptions was installed by The Atlantic Journal. Pipes for the purpose of sewage disposal were being planned by the Chelsea Beach Company when rights were granted for the service in the Chelsea section of the city.

1889

September is historically the height of the so-called "hurricane" season at the shore and Sunday, September 9th, 1889, became a day to remember for thousands of residents and visitors in Atlantic City. According to statistics, it was just about the worst hurricane ever to hit Absecon Island, including those in modern times. Its force wrecked most of the boardwalk and countless buildings on it. Many caught fire and burned to the ground because firefighters were unable to reach the scene, due to the depth of the water, which was two and three feet deep. At Georgia Avenue, the ocean and bay met, and in many places depths of six feet and more were recorded, necessitating the rescue of many people by boat. There were no trains in or out of the resort for days! The water main across the meadows was shut off and the only supply for three days was from artesian wells. Many homes were simply washed away with scarcely a trace but, so far as we can learn, there was, miraculously, no loss of life attributed to the big blow.

Our city was among the first in the nation to install an electric fire alarm system, and it was officially dedicated and put into operation in June of 1889. It was first used for a chimney fire at the Shelburne Hotel that August. A new "Seaview Excursion House" was established on the beach, just west of Albany Avenue, in an effort to popularize the area which had been newly opened for development. Folks who arrived in town on the excursion trains didn't go very much for the idea of being so far downtown, and lots of them took the electric trolleys, which had started running down that far in June of 1889. They'd spend the day around the old site at Missouri Avenue and up toward the piers.

Ten years later the Seaview was sold for other purposes, after failing to enjoy the success anticipated a decade earlier.

The Cordery brothers, John and Samuel, of Absecon, had leased a right-of-way over the railroad tracks to run horse cars between South Carolina Avenue and the Inlet on Atlantic Avenue. William Bartlett bought out the Corderys and substituted mules for horses. Later, the railroad company refused to extend the lease and took over the street cars, extending the service to the Seaview Excursion House, then at Missouri and Pacific Avenues. On May 10, 1889, the mule cars ceased operation.

1890

36 years after the incorporation of Atlantic City, a single track railroad line was opened by the Brigantine Beach Railroad Company, from Brigantine Junction near Pomona, connecting with the Reading tracks. The line ran through Oceanville and was about 14 miles long with a station on Shore Road. It boasted a trestle 2,000 feet long across Grassy Bay, between Trowser's Creek and 2nd Street in Brigantine. In 1903, this trestle collapsed during an extremely high storm tide and service to Brigantine Island ended, except by boat across the bay. A year later all service between Oceanville and Brigantine Junction was halted and the tracks were torn up.

Brigantine Island, just to the north of Absecon Island, is named for a type of vessel which plied the oceans of the world in those days, and many of them went to watery graves on the shoals off the island, more than 200 years ago. Their rotted remains lie on the bottom today, awaiting the arrival of divers to see what treasure they can retrieve from their ancient cargoes.

Old records show that Brigantine was once two separate islands divided by Quarter's Inlet, long since removed by the action of Mother Nature. The section nearest Atlantic City was first called Peters' Beach after the man who made the initial survey in 1724. Originally incorporated as the Borough of Brigantine Beach on June 3, 1890, the community's first Mayor was Alfred B. Smith. Its present day mayor is John Rogge. On April 23, 1897, it was re-incorporated as Brigantine City. Then, in 1914, on April 9th, the city underwent another change, this time to "East Atlantic City"! In 1924, the name was changed again to the present "City of Brigantine". A modern highway bridge, the Justice Vincent Haneman

The United States Hotel, from which States Avenue received its name. Photo re-copy by Harold J. Swartz.

Bridge, illuminated at night, now connects it with Atlantic City, replacing the old wooden span which was washed away more than once during devastating Atlantic storms.

States Avenue, once the proud address of many beautiful guest houses and hotels, is the former location of the old mule tramway from the United States Hotel to the beach. States Avenue was officially dedicated by John S. Davis, owner of the United States Hotel, on June 16, 1890. Wealthy residents objected to its paving because they preferred the street to have a gravel surface for their horses! They held out until 1948 when States Avenue finally was paved!

The very first street in our city to be paved was South Carolina Avenue, between Arctic and Atlantic Avenues, in January of 1890. Material used was brick. Our boardwalk was moved further seaward due to beach accretion on at least two occasions, the first being in 1890, when the line of the fourth boardwalk was set out in the section between North Carolina and New York Avenues, about a hundred feet. The second time was in 1907, when the boardwalk was widened to 40 feet, between Connecticut and Rhode Island Avenues. In February of 1890, City Council announced that there would be no further boardwalk construction from Massachusetts Avenue to Caspian, nor from Florida to Morris Avenues, until property owners agreed not to erect any buildings outside the 'walk. All but two of the owners signed the agreement. Those two, William Bowker, at Mississippi Avenue, and Richard H. Lee, at Texas Avenue, had small piers outside the boardwalk. It was not until after the turn of the century that litigation decided once and for all who was right and who was not. Meanwhile, Bowker and Lee shut off the boardwalk at their lines, defying the city, and their properties became known as Fort Bowker and Fort Lee! The census of 1890 showed our town had grown to 13,055 souls!

1891

Nowhere on earth, say world travelers, does a seashore resort boast so large and so efficient a force for the protection of its bathers as does the Atlantic City Beach Patrol, founded August 24, 1891. Public demand caused the city to authorize the organization of the patrol for duty during the so-called "bathing hours" of 9 a.m. to 5 p.m., rather than during the hours around noon. Originally, 10 policemen had been assigned to this work, but for the season of 1892, 20 lifeguards, fully trained for their duties, were hired by the city. Ten lifeboats were made available that first season. Volunteer guards, however, continued in sections not covered by the regulars for a number of years. The most colorful was said to have been Captain Charles Clark, a former cowboy, who wore a velvet coat and went around most of the time with a ring buoy over his shoulder, which carried his name emblazoned in large letters! Clark claimed to have rescued some 700 persons, in his years on the beach, and was known as "The Velvet-Coated Hero." He passed on in 1918.

Atlantic City boasted 28 grocery stores in 1891, nine photographer's shops, three jewelry shops, 64 hotels and guest houses, eight confectionaries, eight bakeries, two cycle shops, four shoe stores, two plumbers, nine real estate and insurance firms, two ice and coal companies, one furniture store, one laundry, and believe it or not, only two restaurants! There was only one printer in our town at that time, only one blacksmith, one 5&10 cent store, and one liquor store. And to take care of the ills of the residents, we had nine pharmacies.

Two of the popular songs of the day were "Down Went McGinty" (To the Bottom of the Sea) and "O, Promise Me".

Atlantic City, N. J.

U. S. Life Savers in Action

Arrived safe and sound. The place is fine. Dear love.

Published by American Novelty Co., 143 So. Virginia Avenue, Atlantic City, N. J.

1892

The area around Pennsylvania and Virginia Avenues, on either side of Steel Pier, seems to have always been a popular bathing spot. Old records list Adams' Baths and Jackson's Baths as two of the most well-known such facilities, in 1892. Old post cards in my collection portray huge crowds on those beaches posing for the photographer during summer outings. An old copy of the Atlantic City Press carries an ad, stating that Alfred Adams Jr. was "Bathmaster" and the fee was 50¢ per week. With your own suit, that is! Was this an early form of beach fee or was it a charge made by Adams' Baths for people to change into bathing attire?

Jackson Baths, Pennsylvania Avenue and the Boardwalk, boasted accommodations for 100 bathers, as well as a number of apartments, and restrooms with cots for the use of bathers. Jackson's was considered, at that time, to be just about the best-equipped bathouse on the Atlantic Coast!

During the "Gay 90's", some bicycles used on the streets of our city had a huge front wheel and a small rear one, but these were soon replaced by what was called the "safety", which resembled our present day bicycles, except that they had only one speed and they were much more difficult to pedal! The origin of the name is obvious . . . they were much safer than their high old predecessors.

13

Published by Hubin's Big Post Card Store, Atlantic City.

The first real theatre on the Atlantic City boardwalk was the Academy of Music at New York Avenue. It had been erected by Joseph Fralinger to house a trained horse show, with the fancy name of "Bartholomew's Equine Paradox", but when the act took to the road in 1892, the building was remodeled and became a theatre. However, the structure burned to the ground, in June of that year. The owners were not the least bit dismayed, and certainly must have been covered by insurance because it was rebuilt in the amazingly short time of four weeks and became a top house for great shows. But, believe it or not, fire struck again in 1898, and this time it was rebuilt of brick, only to be gutted by the great fire of 1902, that took a heavy toll along our boardwalk.

The dauntless owners remodeled the theatre, gave it a brand new name and it opened in April of 1908 as the Apollo, which was to become the top legitimate theatre in town, and the break-in spot for many pre-Broadway shows. After an illustrious career of providing stellar entertainment, the Apollo became a moving picture theatre in 1924.

The Electrical Bureau, which takes care of fire alarms, traffic lights and the maintenance and construction of the city's street lighting, was founded by a man named Dahlgren Albertson in 1892, and it operated out of City Hall. Willard Wright returned as Mayor through 1893.

The United States Hotel was taken over by John S. Davis and Elwood Jones that year, and they cut the land up into cottage sites, moving the hotel to the Pacific Avenue side of the square. The original wing of the hostelry contained 125 rooms and the Atlantic Avenue addition brought the total number to 225. During its early years, the United States hotel played host to many prominent visitors including senators, editors, congressmen, lawyers, authors and captains of industry. It was surrounded by trees and landscaped gardens, and was truly the resort of the elite of early day Atlantic City.

1893

The phrase "No Snow On The Boardwalk" is one which is steeped in tradition. It has been printed and reprinted and used in advertising brochures for years. The earliest record of snow removal from our wooden way is dated January 8, 1893, when City Council ordered that snow be cleared from the boardwalk at a cost of $10. At that time, $10 would pay 10 men for a 12-hour day! Among the early devices used to do the job, was a plow with a wooden blade, so it could not harm the surface of the 'walk. Now the job is done by mechanized equipment. Crews are out early, often while the snow still falls, so as to keep intact that old boast "No Snow On The Boardwalk" and promenaders can enjoy an invigorating stroll, regardless of the weather. But the practice has a more practical purpose. Should a fire break out in any of our boardwalk buildings, fire fighting equipment would be badly hampered by snow if it could not move freely along the boards. So it's a safety measure as well.

The infamous Panic of 1893 swept the nation that year, and Atlantic City felt its effect. Visitors were fewer in number and money was in short supply. However, plans went ahead for the improvement of Atlantic City, if not in physical form, at least on paper and in the minds of the leaders of business and industry, who had faith that better days were on the way. Two steamers used for fishing trips operated out of Young's Pier. They were the "Nada" and the "Stoy". A 50-passenger car, which ran on tracks, transported the passengers right out to the boats!

William Somers, a local man, had built a successful "observation wheel", and with the opening of the World's Fair in Chicago in '93, the Somers Company applied for space, but a Mr. Ferris, who owned a huge wheel constructed of steel, received permission from the city for the use of the entire fair ground area where the amusement rides were located, and this resulted in the management's relegating Somers' wooden observation wheel to the area outside the fair itself. Yet, it attracted many fearless riders and the patent from the invention of William Somers, here in Atlantic City, resulted in many such observation wheels being erected at amusement centers in many cities.

In his "Book of the Boardwalk", author Frank Butler states that today's Ferris Wheel really should be called the "Somers Wheel" since it is identical to that local man's invention except for the material used in construction.

Franklin P. Stoy was Mayor of Atlantic City, and City Hall Annex opened in December with apartments and stores. It was located at Tennessee and Atlantic Avenues. This followed the disastrous fire of August, 1893, which also destroyed the Opera House and two adjoining buildings on Atlantic Avenue. Incidentally, a lot at Tennessee and Atlantic was secured by the city in a rather unusual way. Patrick O'Reilly, a Pennsylvanian, owned quite a bit of property in our city and owed several years back taxes. As settlement, O'Reilly consented to deed to the city that 125-foot-front lot in lieu of taxes, in the amount of about $2,500. 30 years later, the lot had increased in value nearly 400 percent and was worth approximately $90,000!

1894

A Pleasantville inventor, Captain Amariah Lake, had a unique idea for a new amusement called "The Haunted Swing", which operated for some years in Atlantic City at States Avenue and the Boardwalk. The swing, fashioned like a flat-bottomed boat, carried about 20 persons and was suspended inside a room resembling a living room. When filled with happy passengers, the swing was given a start by an attendant, who then left the room, and the swing apparently moved faster and faster til it seemed to go over the bar on which it was suspended! Passengers held on for dear life, laughing and screaming with glee, but often, in fright! Actually the swing remained stationary, while the room revolved! All the furniture was securely fastened to the walls and floor. Patrons of this early day "ride" had a ball, and made The Haunted Swing one of the most popular amusements in town! Meanwhile, James Cathcart and William Oswald erected a similar attraction on the 'walk near Arkansas Avenue, even then an area for much concentration of leisure time enterprises. Cathcart's and Oswald's brain child was arranged amid a forest and garden setting. It had mirrors that gave customers the sensation of swinging and the forest was filled with singing birds, blooming plants and other decorations, creating the appearance of something right out of Grimm's Fairy Tales! We wonder how many people now would pay for a ride on such an amusement in today's sophisticated society! Back then, folks found enjoyment in simple ways and didn't care about flashing lights, loud music and such! But they loved sitting in a room that revolved, even though they knew they were being fooled!

William Somers continued his activity in the field of amusements and his carrousel, near New York Avenue, was 80 feet in diameter, with three decks! On the first were animals; on the second, a roller skating rink, while the top deck was a dance floor complete with orchestra! It could accommodate 1,500 persons! That year, a contract was let for the construction of three steamboats for service between Longport, Ocean City and Somers Point. They went into operation the following year. The distance between the landing pavilion at 16th Street in Longport and the wharf at 2nd Street in Ocean City was two-and-three-quarters miles. At Longport, on the southernmost tip of Absecon Island, an extension 36 by 50 feet was added as well as a floating dock. The pier also had a restaurant, ticket office and railroad freight station. Strong currents around the Longport Pier had presented problems for years, and in 1899, the structure had to be strengthened by placing reinforcements around the base of the pilings.

Although no time tables have been located, it is believed that service between Longport and Ocean City was maintained hourly, connecting with scheduled trains. Boats ran only during the summer months, June through mid-September. However, in later years the steamboats also operated at Eastertime, which then, as now, attracted thousands to the Boardwalk to parade in their spring finery. And, wherever people gathered for a song or two, one was almost certain to hear these current favorites: "I Don't Want To Play In Your Yard", and "The Sidewalks of

New York."

Siracusa Insurance Company, sponsor of this book, was founded in 1894, by Antonio S. Siracusa, who had emigrated to this country from Sicily, four years earlier.

The World Post Card Co. 1008 Walnut St., Phila., Pa.

1895

"Having wonderful time. Wish you were here." That timeless message has been mailed from Atlantic City on millions of post cards since the idea for the cards was brought back from Germany by the wife of a local printer! Mrs. Carl Voelker, Sr., was travelling abroad and noticed a new method of writing to friends. It was a picture post card and it was really catching on in Europe! Upon her arrival home, Mrs. Voelker presented the idea to her husband, who agreed to approach several local hotels with the idea of using post cards as advertising pieces. The trend became so popular that thousands of "view cards", as they were called, were printed here and mailed for one cent each all over the nation and the world! The "penny post card" became a popular item and the first thing one did upon arriving at the shore was buy a selection of post cards to send to the folks back home. Colorful picture post cards of our hotels, piers and boardwalk were available at many locations, but one of the largest selections of cards was that at Hubin's Big Post Card Store, 813 Boardwalk.

Prior to World War I, a large percentage of our cards were printed in Germany from photographs made here. As a deltiologist, the name given to collectors of post cards, I have in my collection hundreds of views of early day Atlantic City, including many hotels and other buildings that have been razed to make way for progress. But they live on, on these pieces of cardboard, thanks to an idea brought back from Germany by Mrs. Voelker in 1895!

Published by Sithens Post Card Co., Atlantic City, N. J.

One of our famous landmarks, The Skytower at Central Pier, had a predecessor 'way back in 1895. Known as the "Revolving Observation Tower" it was one of the many inventions of Jesse Lake, of Pleasantville. In fact, there were two of these towers on the Atlantic City beach at that time: one at Massachusetts Avenue, and the other at New York Avenue. They were made of steel and stood 125 feet high. A circular elevator carried people on an enclosed platform, which revolved around the tower and was slowly drawn to a height of 103 feet, affording passengers a fine view of Absecon Island and all the ships at sea. For a thrilling 10-minute ride, the cost was one thin dime!

A near tragedy occurred that year when "The Casino", at Baltic Avenue and the Boardwalk, a two-story dance hall and store, collapsed on July 10th, as pilings gave way under the weight of a huge crowd attending an Elks' Convention. The excited stomping of feet by hundreds of people listening to a speech by Grand Exalted Ruler M. D. Detweiler was blamed. No fatalities resulted, but there were some broken arms and legs and other injuries.

1896

This year marked the construction of the fifth, and present boardwalk. Promenaders increased to such a large number that city fathers decided to again widen the 'walk and an entirely new boardwalk opened July 8th, from Chelsea to Rhode Island Avenues. The dedication was the biggest event this resort had ever seen. Mrs. Franklin P. Stoy, wife of our Mayor, completed the job by driving a golden spike. That spike was covered by a metal plate to prevent theft but it was later stolen and so far as is known, was never recovered. Our boardwalk was now 40 feet wide, standing on steel pilings with steel girders. It also featured heavy steel railings, something that had been missing on previous boardwalks.

The second worst railroad wreck, in the history of New Jersey, occurred July 30th, at the meadow crossing of the Pennsylvania and Reading Railroads, one mile outside the city limits. A Reading Flyer rammed the center of a Redmen's Lodge excursion train from Cumberland and Salem Counties, due to a mix-up in signals, killing 60 persons and injuring 100 others!

What may have been the first air-conditioned theatre in the nation was the "Empire" on Atlantic Avenue which opened July 1st, with a cooling system fed by a central plant with underground pipes carrying a refrigerant similar to that in use today. Not enough customers could be signed up by the firm which supplied the service, the Atlantic City Cooling Company, and it went out of business.

"South Atlantic City" was a lively place in 1896! Where was South Atlantic City? Just where the name indicates: near the southern end of Absecon Island. The name later was changed to Margate City. According to a long-time resident of the area who lived there as a young woman, the old Elephant Hotel and the Mansion House were popular gathering places, each with its own orchestra to entertain the fun-loving crowds. She told us that the dance hall at the Elephant Hotel was known as the Turkish Pavilion and was built just back of the Elephant, so it appeared as if it were being pulled along like a chariot by the huge pachyderm! The hall was garishly decorated with pennants, bunting and bright paint schemes. Steam trains stopped at Lennig's Station. Mr. Lennig, a member of a prominent Philadelphia family, owned much property in South Atlantic City. Coolidge Avenue was then called Jackson Avenue, according to our informant, and the only area settled and sort of "built up" was from Jackson to Washington Avenues, then a few blocks up around the Elephant. The remainder of the area consisted of dunes and underbrush.

Along the beach, birds had dropped seeds and these had flourished and grown into bushes and trees. This was called "Cedar Grove". A hotel was erected there which lured the fashionable folk of the period to its dance floor and other attractions. A post office was needed, so one was established in the Aberdeen Hotel. Alice J. Whittaker was its first postmistress, in 1896. In summer, with the influx of visitors, a branch office was in operation at the Elephant Hotel. Later, the Post Office occupied a building at Jefferson and Atlantic Avenues, along with a store which carried general merchandise. That end of the island already was bustling with activity as residents and visitors recognized its potential and land developers already were looking at it with sincere interest.

That year saw a major fire in Atlantic City when ten dwellings, located 119 to 137 Natter's Alley, were destroyed, on Christmas Day! Some of the popular songs included "Mother Was A Lady", "She May Have Seen Better Days", "A Hot Time In The Old Town Tonight", "The Band Played On", and "She's Only A Bird In A Gilded Cage."

1897

Many of you will remember the talented sand artists who plied their trade on the beaches of Atlantic City until the early forties. They would work in the sand along the railing of the Boardwalk, creating beautiful sculptures that were really lifelike. Their pay? Coins tossed down to them by interested spectators! The first known sand artist on the beach here was Philip McCord, in 1897. Where he learned the art is not known. From then until 1944, when the practice was abolished by City Commission following the hurricane, people would stand fascinated, watching the deft hands of the sand artists create all manner of objects, held together by what was said to be a secret substance, the basis of which was simply beach sand. Among their creations were animals, fish, historical scenes, automobiles, people and various intricate designs.

American Novelty Co., 143 So. Virginia Avenue, Atlantic City, N. J.

Published by Frank B. Hubin's Big Post Card Store, 813 Boardwalk, Atlantic City, N. J., Copyright 1907.

The extension of Atlantic Avenue to Jackson Avenue, which marks the city limits, was made along the old railroad right-of-way in January and the bend in Atlantic Avenue at Boston, which makes it the first street from the ocean the rest of the way downbeach, was caused by its following the original right-of-way of the Camden and Atlantic Railroad. The first building designed exclusively for post office use in Atlantic City, was erected by James Lafferty, at 17 South New York Avenue, in 1897. The postmaster then was Michael Devine.

It is believed that this year marked the first showing of moving pictures at a theatre on the boardwalk: the Corbett-Fitzsimmons Heavyweight Championship bout on March 17, shown at the States Avenue Opera House and at the American Biograph.

Our town has weathered many a severe storm, and according to a newspaper account of the 1930's, the year 1897 saw at least two violent storms rip Atlantic City and the surrounding area. In October, a nor'easter hit and lasted for several days. All rail and wire communication was cut off and relatives of the estimated 10,000 visitors in town were frantic with worry. Tides covered the meadows, with huge whitecaps rolling there. Finally, a stalwart band of men ventured across the water-covered expanse to Pleasantville, following the railroad bed, and brought word to the outside world that Atlantic City was safe, if uncomfortable. Then, the following month, a two-day snowstorm started on November 26, dumping 12 inches of the white stuff on the resort.

Among the popular songs of that year were "Asleep in the Deep", "Just Break the News to Mother", "On the Banks of the Wabash" and "Sweet Rosie O'Grady".

Ball Room on Ocean end of Steel Pier, Atlantic City, N. J.

1898

The famous Steel Pier, at Virginia Avenue and the Beach, first opened for the season of 1898, having been built at a cost of $200,000! It was then the most expensive of all the ocean piers and quickly became the "in" spot of Atlantic City. The big pier featured afternoon and evening concerts, headlined by the cream of the nation's top performers. When one visited Steel Pier in those days, one dressed for the occasion and it was quite beneficial to one's social status to be seen on the pier at one of the performances of a name star. We'll be doing a lot of reminiscing about the great Steel Pier as the years roll by, and take a look at some of the great stars who played that famous showplace that was to become known as "The Amusement City at Sea".

American Novelty Co., 143 So. Virginia Avenue, Atlantic City, N. J.

When what is now the Atlantic City Medical Center opened as the Atlantic City Hospital in 1898, the building was almost entirely furnished and one patient was already installed! On opening day, November 30, the public was invited to inspect the facilities between 10 AM and 10 PM. During the winter of 1896-97, a fund of $529 had been raised, largely through the efforts of Miss Josephine O'Brien. A Women's Auxiliary was organized at the Hotel Dennis, in 1897, and its members collected some $600. Prior to this, such movements had met with many obstacles and much discouragement, and money raised often did not reach the treasury of the organization but went for some other use.

Mrs. Edward Semple was also instrumental in founding the hospital, collecting money which she personally guarded until she was certain it would be used for its intended purpose. A newspaper account on the opening, published the following day, lists donations of soap, towels, and even "a case of liquors for medicinal purposes".

Mrs. Mary Kimmell was its first superintendent, and physicians on duty at its opening were Doctors Clyde M. Fish and Emory Marvel. An early report states that about half the cost of maintaining the hospital was borne by the city and the remainder by individuals.

Published by I. & M. Ottenheimer, Baltimore, Maryland.

The Beach Pirates Chemical Engine Company, which had been formed in 1895, suffered embarrassment when their own firehouse burned in October, 1898, while the company was off battling a blaze between South Carolina and Tennessee Avenues. This was a devastating fire which swept the Somers Casino and Palace, Circle Merry-Go-Rounds, Moore's and the Palace Baths, the Dewey and Hudson Hotels, Schwab's Hotel and Rathskeller, Freisinger's Art Store, Thesan's Turkish Goods, five dwellings and 11 other buildings, including the Beach Pirates' own firehouse! They took the incident in stride and set about rebuilding as soon as the ashes cooled. Our mayor then was Joseph Thompson.

If you're a rail buff, the following, gleaned from a book published in that era, called "Atlantic City and County", should really interest you. Angus Sinclair, noted authority on speed, is quoted in the book as writing "The fastest train in the world runs from Camden to Atlantic City, a distance of 55.5 miles in 50 minutes, for an average speed of 62.2 miles per hour. The engine was hauling seven cars, each averaging 75,000 pounds. The engineer was Charles H. Fahl and the fireman was John Pettit". Mr. Sinclair rode in the cab with the fireman. Fuel was, of course, coal, in small lumps similar to that used for heating homes.

He told of speeding past farms, through scrub pine and oak and over sandy terrain. About four miles from Atlantic City, he wrote, a signal was against the train and speed was reduced to about 20 miles an hour. Two minutes were used in running the last two miles through switches. Even with deductions, Sinclair calculated the average run was made at a speed of more than 70 miles an hour!

Shiloh Baptist Church, Ohio and Arctic Avenues, was erected in 1898, and stands today. Some of the songs which had people humming and singing back then include "She's More To Be Pitied Than Censured", "Gypsy Love Song" and "She Was Bred In Old Kentucky."

1899

While browsing through a copy of "The Atlantic Review" of August 31, 1899, we note that there was open gambling on Absecon Island at that time, so it seems there is really nothing new under the sun! One item in that publication tells of a female reporter riding on an open trolley car to what she called "South Atlantic City", now Margate, to an old mansion named Monte Carlo. There she watched many important, well-to-do citizens engaged in playing races, Faro and roulette. She described the scene as one of excitement and merriment. The story has no by-line but the woman apparently was one of the first members of the distaff side to work as a newspaper reporter in our town!

Certain resort hotelmen were being arrested for holding the baggage of many of their guests when complaints were made about food and service! When such guests asked to check out, the inn keepers reportedly threatened to hold their luggage unless they paid for a full week's stay! And that often amounted to as much as $60 or $70!

The weather, then as now, was an important factor topic of the day, and there is an item in "The Atlantic Review", relating how bad weather had affected yachting at the Inlet. And an ad in that paper offers a new gas range at cost, including hookup at no charge, by a local appliance firm.

It was a time for real enjoyment in the Queen of Resorts, with all sorts of diversions listed in the newspaper, including the Academy of Music at New York Avenue and the Boardwalk; the Inlet Pavilion "At the Terminus of the Electric Railway"; baseball at Inlet Park, featuring the Atlantic City Collegians versus Allentown, Pennsylvania.

Other attractions included The Moorish Palace, Boardwalk at New York Avenue; The Blue Cavern Grotto; Rudolf's Grotto Cafe; The Wonderful Myriad Dances at 10¢ admission; The London Ghost Show "at the foot of States Avenue"; The Empire Theatre, 1523 Atlantic, Henry Keunhle, Manager; Doyle's Pavilion, Boardwalk at Missouri; Guvernator's Mammoth Pavilion, Boardwalk below Arkansas Avenue, with its "Continuous High Class Vaudeville" and Locheil Summer Garden, 15 S. Delaware

Avenue. And, oh yes . . . there was "The Grand Cakewalk Dance Contest" held nightly on Young's Million Dollar Pier!

The Auditorium Pier Company began construction of a pier at the ocean end of Pennsylvania Avenue to house a large theatrical house. The city refused to permit its connection to the boardwalk because it was not the specified one-thousand feet long as required in the easement deeds,which the firm claimed did not apply to this property. Legal action ensued, delaying the opening until August. 1899 saw the first brick hotels on the boardwalk: The Waldorf-Astoria and Bleak House, each six stories high and located at the west and east corners respectively, of Ocean Avenue. The Waldorf was built by Wilden Moore; Bleak House by Captain John Young, Clarence Busch and William Loudenslager.

The Atlantic City Horse Show was formed at a meeting held in the Windsor Hotel in April. G. Jason Waters, with whom the idea originated, was elected president. The purpose of the association was to stage an annual horse show which would attract leading owners and others interested in fine equines and equipages. The first of these shows was held July 13, 14 and 15, at Inlet Park and proved to be an instant success! The exhibits included roadsters, hackneys, horses in harness, saddle horses, polo ponies, hunters and jumpers, four-in-hands, fire horses and apparatus, hotel coaches and delivery wagons. Some of the important names on the show roster in addition to its president were Charles Evans, Allen B. Endicott, Walter J. Buzby, Joseph Thompson, F. W. Hemsley, J. H. Lippincott, H. W. Leeds, D. S. White, Jacob Myers, Edward S. Lee, A. O. Dayton, Josiah White, J. B. Reilly, Charles Lacey and John G. Shreve.

Easter Sunday, 1899 fell on April 2 and saw one of the greatest crowds in the city's history, up to that time, great in fact, even by today's standards! The weather was not what one would call ideal. It was chilly and raw with a snow squall thrown in for good measure. Nonetheless, between 11 A.M. and 1 P.M., the number of promenaders was the largest of the day, with two steady streams of people heading in each direction that reached from rail to rail. Then, between 4 and 5 P.M. the walk was again packed with humanity across its entire width. Trains into the resort pulled as many as 25 cars and arrived in many sections. Meanwhile, back on the boardwalk, just about every rolling chair available was pressed into service being pushed single file with no interference to strollers." Needless to say, beer gardens, soda pop emporiums and hot dog stands had a busy day!

By 1899, the capacity of the Children's Seashore House was 100 children and 30 mothers. Those who were able to afford it, paid board at the rate of $3 per week, which included medical attendance and laundry. Railroad tickets were also furnished at reduced rates.

Some of the top songs in that bygone year were, "The Band Played On", "Hearts and Flowers", "The Moth and The Flame", "My Wild Irish Rose", "Hello My Baby", "When You Were Sweet 16", and "You Tell Me Your Dream, I'll Tell You Mine."

EXCURSION HOUSE

CHILDRENS SEA SHORE HOUSE

No Publisher listed.

1900

The Press Club of Atlantic City was founded this year. Such organizations had been formed earlier but broke up for some reason or other. The longest-lived of those forerunners to The Press Club was probably the Journalists' Club, organized in the late 90's. Strangely enough, its membership included many local celebrities, judges, physicians, lawyers, hotelmen and others. And, oh yes . . . some newspapermen! Next came the Pen and Pencil Club, but it, too, failed to survive.

Shortly after the turn of the century, Mayor Franklin P. Stoy suggested to some of his friends in the newspaper fraternity that a good press club would be an asset to the resort and could benefit its members in many ways, so on May 16, 1900, The Press Club of Atlantic City was organized with 13 members. Mayor Stoy served as its first president. The following month, the club sponsored a huge coaching parade, comprised of more than a hundred horse-drawn vehicles traveling from Atlantic City to Longport for the dedication of the New Longport Speedway. And the summer of 1900 saw the first 4th of July celebration in many years in our town. And it, too, was sponsored by the young and enthusiastic Press Club of Atlantic City, still going strong 80 years later!

The Longport Speedway was gravel-surfaced and provided a good road for the fancy horse-drawn rigs of the day as well as the "Wheelman", a well known group of bicyclists. It later became Ventnor Avenue and is known to have been used quite often as a speedway in modern times. The artery actually was begun in 1899, and finished in just about a year, not bad time considering the lack of mechanized equipment. True, there was some machinery in use but the greater part of the labor was done by men with strong backs, using the old fashioned pick and shovel, along with a lot of honest sweat!

The Consumers' Gas Company opened a plant on Florida Avenue, and that building, along with another on Michigan Avenue, was purchased by Clarence H. Geist, in 1909, and merged into the Atlantic City Gas Company. Gas lights were in evidence all around the city, having been placed on our streets in 1880, but they still were a novelty to many of our visitors who hailed from rural areas and small towns, which had no such "modern" lighting.

Close harmony was very popular with Barbershop Quartets rendering such ballads as "My Wild Irish Rose", "Take Back Your Gold" and "Tell Me Pretty Maiden, Are There Any More At Home Like You?"

The Atlantic City Public Library first opened on January 31, 1900, in the Rochford Sanitorium, Mt. Vernon and Pacific Avenues, with just 197 books on its shelves, the result of a book reception at the Hotel Dennis the preceding June. In October, the first librarian, a Miss Evans, resigned and Miss Rena Somers was appointed to take her place. The library flourished and grew, and in six months there were 435 patrons. An earlier attempt at establishing a library here was made in 1891, but it failed about six months later because few people took advantage of it. There had been a couple of reading rooms but the first effort to establish a full-fledged library was made in 1900 by that group of ladies from the Research Club.

1901

The first Christmas Club in the nation was established by a gentleman named Byron Sharp, a shipping clerk in Philadelphia, who decided this would be a good method of saving money for a seashore vacation in Atlantic City. He talked up his idea to a couple of bankers and the rest is history!

A local man, Samuel Headley, drove a horse and wagon door-to-door at about this time selling fresh milk, after loading up at his Fairmount Avenue headquarters. A woman, who recalls how delicious that milk tasted, told me that one could purchase as little as 2¢ worth if one supplied their own container! Skim milk sold for 4¢ a quart; regular was 8¢! Local folks would wait for Headley's wagon to come along and he'd ladle out the desired amount with his big dipper. This lady told me that later in the decade, the Wilson Dairy Milk Depot on South New York Avenue, operated a small stand where one could buy a glass of fresh, cold milk for a nickel!

Josiah White, with his son John, formed a company to purchase a site for a hotel between Park Place and Ohio Avenue, then occupied by the Academy of the Sacred Heart. The following year, Marlborough House was built and the hostelry won immediate acceptance from vacationers who were looking for lodgings that left nothing to be desired.

The census current at that time, which had been taken in 1900, showed Atlantic City with 27,838 residents. Brigantine had 99. The Borough of Longport had only 80, while South Atlantic City, now Margate, boasted a population of 69!

City Council was urged by a group of local people who favored a free library, to put the matter up to the voters. This was done on February 11, 1901, and the library was adopted by a vote of 6062 to 30! Five trustees were duly appointed and the Atlantic City free Public Library was on its way!

Captain John L. Young build a brick, 7-story apartment house on the Boardwalk at Tennessee Avenue, containing 112 units. And the reverse of today's conversions of apartments into condominiums happened, the apartment building eventually becoming Young's Hotel. Later, it was to undergo a series of name changes including the Alamac, Knickerbocker and Mayflower, home of the famous "Holiday Room" where thousands of people had such wonderful times in the 40's and 50's.

1902

One of the worst fires in Boardwalk history occurred on April 3, 1902, when a blaze broke out at Illinois Avenue. The resulting inferno destroyed every building along the 'walk between Illinois and New York Avenues, with one lone exception, The Academy of Music, which was built of brick! Embers blown through the air ignited Young's Pier at Tennessee Avenue, causing some damage there. In all 12 hotels and four bathhouses were destroyed: The Bryn Mawr, Berkeley, Evard, Kenilworth, Luray, Mervine, Norwood, New Holland, Rio Grande, Stratford, Stickney and Tarleton, plus the Adams, Brady, Carr and Mervine Bath Houses, as well as 23 other business establishments, and two homes.

In April, the Atlantic City Public Library moved to the third floor of the old City Hall, with members of the Women's Research Club serving as librarians, without pay. Later in the year, the City took over a building on the site of the present library, at Illinois and Pacific Avenues, and it opened to the public on New Year's Day, 1903!

One of Atlantic City's most beautiful hotels had its beginning as Marlborough House in 1902. Many innovations were featured at the new hostelry, including an ice water system with outlets in every room, an idea which had been successful earlier in a Philadelphia office building. The Marlborough was later joined by the Blenheim, and together they survived until 1978, when they were demolished to make way for Bally Corporation's beautiful new "Park Place" Casino Hotel complex. A number of artifacts from the Old Marlborough Blenheim were saved and have been incorporated into the decor of Park Place as a reminder of Atlantic City's opulent past.

This was the year the famed "Floradora Sextette" of lovely dancers appeared at George C. Tilyou's Pier, backed musically by, believe it or not, John Philip Sousa's Concert Band! Song hits of the day included "In The Good Old Summer Time", "On a Sunday Afternoon", and 'Under The Bamboo Tree".

A bicycle race track, the Velodrome, opened on Connecticut Avenue, just off the boardwalk, in April. A board track, it was one of the fastest and safest such tracks of the era, and is said to have continued in operation on and off, until the start of the World War in 1917. Its purses were quite attractive and lured a number of top riders from across the nation as well as from Europe.

A 1902 brochure of the Philadelphia and Reading Railway describes Brigantine as "A charming seaside resort adjoining Atlantic City with an electric railroad running the entire length of the beach, connecting every portion of the island with the railroad to Philadelphia, and also by means of a steel ferryboat to and from Atlantic City, making half-hourly trips during the summer." It continues to tout our sister-resort the next island over, by saying "Those who are fond of shooting and fishing will find this altogether the best place for those sports on the ocean coast".

There are three hotels in Brigantine listed in that old brochure: Holland House, "equipped with electric lights and Artesian well water, E. Mehl, Proprietor"; Brigantine House, kept by A. B. Smith, and the well-known Holdzkom House. Rates ranged from $6 all the way up to $35, and that was per person . . . per week! A number of fine cottages were listed too, which could be rented, fully furnished, from the Brigantine Company at $150 to $250 for the season!

Copyright 1902 by Detroit Photographic Co.

1903

The Banana Boat "Brighton" of the United Fruit Line, ran aground off the Inlet Bar at the end of Pacific Avenue on March 30. Hundreds of residents struggled in the sea and on the beach to get their share of the 26,000 bunches of bananas which had been jettisoned by the crew of the helpless vessel. Bananas were the main fare in hundreds of Atlantic City households for weeks, with some of the salvagers hawking the yellow fruit at 15¢ a bunch. In addition, some 4,000 bags of coconuts were thrown overboard!

Steel pilings and girders were being encased in concrete on our boardwalk to prevent further damage by the corrosion caused by salt water. John Hackney was city engineer and Frank Smathers was district court judge. Our mayor was Franklin P. Stoy.

Local commuters were up in arms over the many excursion trains being run to the shore which often caused them to be half an hour or more

29

late at their places of employment. They didn't object to the excursionists per se, but rather to the railroad company because it loaded passengers bound for the shore on excursion trains, and held up the commuter trains for a later departure.

Another matter concerning train travel appeared in a contemporary newspaper story dealing with women occupying seats in smoking cars. The article reads in part: "They do it out of meanness, just to inconvenience or humiliate the smokers." Another faction contends they want to get near enough to the men smoking to try to convert them. Both are wrong! From careful consideration of the matter, supplemented by numerous experiments, we are led to believe that women sit by smokers because they enjoy the smoke. Not for worlds would they smoke themselves, but the aroma is sweet incense to their nostrils and they gradually become addicted to the habit of inhaling it in this second-hand manner! The article continues "We have observed ladies enter a smoking car and, spurning vacant seats, plump themselves down beside a user of the "weed". If deprived of this enjoyment, they have been known to become fretful and nervous and are not content til they get into a tobacco atmosphere"! How about that . . . back in 1903? You've come a long way baby!

Songsters of that year harmonized on such tunes as "You're The Flower Of My Heart", (Sweet Adeline), "Bedelia" and "March of The Toys".

An early attempt to improve the appearance of our neighborhoods was reportedly made in December of 1903, when the Lenox Avenue League was founded. It was the only group of property owners at the time which was formed for the sole purpose of beautifying the city. Membership was restricted to residents and property owners of Lenox or Iowa Avenues. All that winter they spoke glowingly of their plans to make their little corner of the world something which would become a model for the entire town. The following spring, they planted shade trees on both sides of the street from the boardwalk to the thorofare, erected an approach to the boardwalk and planted a flower bed at the foot of the street!

Reporting on that first meeting of the league, the Atlantic City Daily Press said the movement "would go down in the history of Absecon Island, for it means the beginning of something which will spread to every nook and corner of the Island and would result in the ultimate transportation of a city sadly lacking in pulchritude, into one of stately beauty. The procession toward 'The City Beautiful' has started and it behooves everyone who wants to reach the goal, to get in line. Other sections of the city will follow the example of the Lenox Avenue League". This, back in 1903; sounds like a good idea for today, doesn't it?

1904

Even though our city was incorporated in 1854, there was no paid fire department til an ordinance creating it was approved on April 2, 1904. The department was duly organized two days later. There were more than 300 men, many of whom were prominent in the business life of the community, who belonged to the volunteers. Most of them joined the paid department. The city purchased the volunteers buildings and fire-fighting equipment. Two months prior to the volunteers' being disbanded, 100 of its members had traveled to Baltimore, Maryland, to battle the great fire of February 8, 1904. They took with them a half mile of hose and succeeded in preventing the further spread of the fire in the section to which they were assigned!

The Atlantic City and Suburban Traction Company was incorporated in July of 1904, to build an electric railway from Atlantic City over to Pleasantville, Somers Point and Absecon. The local terminal was located at Florida Avenue and the Boardwalk and cars traveled out Florida then crossed the meadows along Old Turnpike to the Mainland. The branch to Absecon was three miles long and to Somers Point, seven and a half miles. Eight new Brill semi-convertible cars were purchased that year and were dubbed "Jubilee" cars, since Atlantic City was then celebrating its 50th anniversary. Some of them were open on the sides for summer use while others had provision for inclement weather.

Our Golden Anniversary celebration in 1904 was called the Semi-Centennial and was held that summer for a surprisingly short period: June 15 to 18! But many special events were packed into the time alloted. One was a huge floral parade with nearly 100 beautifully decorated rolling chairs, which proceeded along our boardwalk from the lighthouse to Florida Avenue. A reviewing stand was set up at Steel Pier. Another outstanding event during our Semi-Centennial was a mammoth marine parade, directed by Louis Kuehnle, Commodore of the Atlantic City Yacht Club, the host club. It was a spectacle to behold, say oldtimers, with a large number of gaily decorated vessels passing in review close enough to the beach so as to be enjoyed by thousands of people lining the board-walk!

The "Court of Honor", between South Carolina and Tennessee Avenues on Atlantic, as well as the electrical features extending four blocks east and eight blocks west, were illuminated for two hours nightly for the remainder of the summer season.

A Mardi-Gras atmosphere prevailed all over town during the observance with house parties, beach parties, hay rides, picnics, trolley parties, fireworks and special entertainment at the hotels and piers. The directors of the celebration wisely decided to provide diversion for the nighttime hours, by contracting with a New York firm for a great fireworks display, known at that time as "Pyrotechnics", and they set off a spectacular exhibition called "The Last Days of Pompeii" for three nights in succession on the beach between North Carolina and Tennessee Avenues, which attracted thousands.

Our first motorized taxicabs went into operation with Fred Dehn, who had operated horse-drawn cabs for six years, putting two Winton automobiles and a Rambler on the street. In June, 1904, The National Tuberculosis Association was founded in Atlantic City.

That same year, a convention of piano dealers was held here and the new upright and grand pianos so excited the dealers they declared

31

the then-popular square type grands obsolete. To demonstrate their disdain for the outmoded instruments, they lit a huge bonfire on the beach, fuel for which was provided by some 1000 of the Old Square "88's"!

Songs popular that year include "Dear Old Girl" (The Robin Sings Above You), "Give My Regards To Broadway", "Goodbye My Lady Love", "Ida, Sweet as Apple Cider", and "On A Sunday Afternoon."

1905

The idea of a Public Library in our city dates back to 1899 when the Women's Research Club saw the need for such a facility. In 1902, the trustees applied to industrialist Andrew Carnegie who gave them a grant of $60,000, later adding another $11,000. Dedication took place January 2, 1905 with some 2000 persons attending. The exterior of the building has remained almost unchanged. Compare the old photograph below with an actual view today, and you'll agree. Our library is one of the oldest public buildings still used for its original purpose, and remains in good condition after 75 years!

That September, automobile races were run on the beach. For that special event, Meadow Boulevard was temporarily opened with approval by the Board of Chosen Freeholders, then officially dedicated on October 8th. Meadow Boulevard now is known as Albany Avenue Boulevard and is part of the state highway system.

Many of our visitors wanted to see other seaside resorts when they visited Atlantic City, because they didn't know how soon they'd be returning, and to accommodate them, four vessels were in operation between Longport and Ocean City with side trips to Somers Point. All one had to do was catch a trolley at the Boardwalk or on Atlantic Avenue and ride to the southernmost end of Absecon Island to Longport. There, they could board one of those steamboats: the "Avalon", "Longport", "Somers

Published by the Post Card Distributing Co., Atlantic City, N. J.

Point", or "Ocean City". Service between Longport and Somers Point was of less importance than the Ocean City route for many reasons, and was reportedly discontinued as of September 12, 1905.

Prior to the elimination of the Somers Point run, patronage required the addition of a fifth steamboat "The Wildwood", which was acquired in 1905 for about $17,000. She was of wood construction and similar in size to the others: 70 feet long with a 15-foot beam, and a gross tonnage of 21. According to a pamphlet issued that year, service may have been resumed in the summer of 1906, but did not run in 1907, since that is the date the Atlantic City and Shore Railroad's "Fast Line" opened for business into Ocean City.

Made in Germany. A. C. Bosselman & Co., New York.

Tracks were laid on Virginia Avenue, the 1000 block, that year, to carry cars out Virginia and in on South Carolina Avenue. Shuttle cars for many years ran between Atlantic Avenue and the Boardwalk on South Carolina Avenue.

The first motor bus line between Atlantic City and Philadephia is mentioned in the paper under date of September 22nd, 1905. Quoting the item: "A fleet of 60-horsepower buses will be started from Atlantic City to Philadelphia on Monday". No further record of bus service appears in publications of that period, and I question the reference to such great horsepower in an era when engines of 30 and 40 HP were unusual. And in those early days of motoring, the autobus had not been developed to the point where such service over so great a distance was likely to be maintained. Roads were very bad, weather unpredictable and service stations just about non-existent!

The first section of boardwalk stretching beyond the city limits at Jackson Avenue was constructed by the City of Ventnor, which opened four blocks, Jackson to Frankfort Avenues, on May 6, 1905.

The very first electric sign that moved was erected on the Atlantic

City Boardwalk in 1905 by the Gillette Safety Razor Company. It was a phenomenon which became a landmark on the wooden way since it was way ahead of its time.

Songs of the day had a happy, lilting quality as evidenced in "The Whistler and His Dog", "In My Merry Oldsmobile", "Mother Pin A Rose On Me", "Everybody Works But Father", and "I Don't Care", the signature of Actress Eva Tanguay.

1906

The Million Dollar Pier, on the Boardwalk at Arkansas Avenue, first opened for the season of 1906 in mid-July with many V.I.P.'s in attendance. Captain John Young and Mrs. Jane Fortesque, operator of a beer garden on the boardwalk for many years, formed a company to operate the new pier which boasted a skating rink, concert band, net haul, which brought up loads of unusual sea creatures from the ocean's depths, theatres, and more. Among the theatres, the old Hippodrome was probably the most famous where some of the top names in show business trod the boards. Among the luminaries who appeared behind the footlights there were "The Jersey Lily", Lily Langtry, Pat Rooney, Jr., Lillian Russell and Victor McLaglen. But it became most famous as the location of the garish showplace, home of one of its owners, Captain Young.

Of Moorish architecture, the flambouyant white building actually stood out on the pier over the ocean and was dubbed "Number One, Atlantic Ocean". The home was furnished in lovely taste with beautiful appointments, including a garden filled with ornate statues and sculptures. A proud boast of the owners was that there never was any dust on the furniture! Over the years, "#1 Atlantic Ocean" played host to more than a few very important guests, who enjoyed such an unusual home located in such an unlikely place. The home was built in 1906 and torn down in 1953. Captain Young passed on in 1938.

CAPT. YOUNG'S RESIDENCE ON MILLION DOLLAR PIER, ATLANTIC CITY, N. J.

Published by the Post Card Distributing Co., Atlantic City, N. J.

On August 25, with but little notice in the local papers, the Shore Fast Line began operation and for the next 42 years provided dependable, speedy transporation via trolley between Atlantic City and the Shore Road communities on the mainland, and then to Ocean City. Five days after its start, the line was experiencing trouble. It seems the third rail, across the meadows between Absecon Island and the mainland was not functioning right and several of the cars had stalled out and the passengers were obliged to wade through mud and water in the marshes, to the Old Turnpike and then take the Atlantic City and Suburban cars back to Atlantic City! It had growing pains for awhile, but once it got going, the Shore Fast Line became a legend in its own time, and many's the tale that can be told concerning that line! How many of our readers took their best girl to the boardwalk and piers on those old cars, or traveled to school on them?

The firm provided a rather unique service at one time. It owned a funeral car called the "Absequam", used to convey funeral groups, including the mourners and the casket from Atlantic City and Ocean City to the Pleasantville Cemetery. When motor hearses came into general use, it was converted into a parlor car and used regularly on the line.

1906 was the year of what has gone down in the annals of railroading history as "The First Big Electric Wreck". It occurred at approximately 2:30 a.m. on Sunday, October 28, when a three-car train from Camden to Atlantic City,with a three-man crew, ran into a slightly open draw bridge. It happened on the old Pennsy's West Jersey and Seashore Line, which had only recently been electrified. Motorman Walter C. Scott was entitled to the day off but worked voluntarily so that his friend, John E. Holmes, could attend church. In the wreck, the first two cars were entirely submerged, the third partly so!! Scott and 56 passengers perished and 32 were injured. On that railroad, the entire right-of-way was enclosed by wire fencing to prevent people and animals from coming into contact with the highly-charged third rail.

This was also the year of the most famous marine event in local waters up to that time, when the steamer "Cherokee" became stranded in dense fog and a calm sea on the Brigantine Shoals, in January. Crews from both life saving stations in Brigantine under command of J. Frank Smith and John Holdzkom, went aboard but the Captain, his crew and passengers refused to leave the ship. There was only minor damage to the "Cherokee" and no casualties!

The first instance of the illumination of an open highway in South New Jersey was on Albany Avenue Boulevard between Atlantic City and Pleasantville, in August of 1906. 53 electric street lamps were turned on to brighten up the roadway for the automobiles of the day such as Stanley Steamers, Locomobiles, Reos, Fords and Whites whose feeble headlamps needed all the help they could get! This took place just a little under one year after the highway was first opened.

The First Car Out of the Water, Thoroughfare Wreck, Atlantic City, Oct. 28, 1906

Walter Scott

MOTORMAN

No Publisher listed.

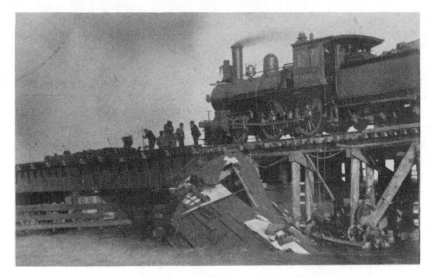

The Dittrich Studios, 1107 Boardwalk, opposite Steeplechase Pier.

1907

Today there are hundreds of them in Atlantic City, but in 1907 there was only one! One what? One taximeter! And that was on an automobile operated as a cab by Charles Lloyd. It wasn't the first taxi but the first to be equipped with a gadget that measured the time and mileage. That same year, the City of Ventnor housed its first piece of motorized fire apparatus in July, the first such equipment on the Island!

Atlantic City engaged the services of the firm of Carrere and Hastings, municipal planning engineers, to submit a plan of improvement for our town. It was laid out and shown to government officials and to the public, but could not be carried out since there appeared to be no means of financing the venture due to its cost, estimated at about $25,000,000! One of its main features was a system of boulevards 135 feet wide!

There were only 142,000 automobiles on the roads of the entire nation then, but Carrere and Hastings' engineers foresaw the need for wider streets, even at that early date. The plan provided for a boulevard running from Maine Avenue to Albany Avenue, to be located about midway between Pacific Avenue and the Boardwalk. Certain phases of the plan were carried out, however, and remain to this day to benefit modern motorists.

That was the year Atlantic City passed the controversial ordinance known as the "Mackintosh Law", which stipulated that if you wore a bathing suit in public, you must also wear an outer garment over it when on local streets. City Council adopted a motion to widen the boardwalk to 40 feet between North Carolina and South Carolina Avenues.

It was also the year a banking institution opened on a seashore boardwalk for the first time in the history of our country! A building was purchased by a local group at the corner of Ocean Avenue, then housing Green's Hotel. After extensive remodeling, it opened for business in July,

37

1907, as The Boardwalk National Bank, now the First National Bank of South Jersey!

The Atlantic City Electric Company took over all local electric supply on the Island in September and the Brigantine Transit Company sold their steamers "Lorraine", "Katherine" and "Brigantine" at auction, in February.

Smith E. Johnson was serving his second term as Sheriff and hit songs of that wonderful year include "School Days", "Red Wing", "On The Road To Mandalay", "Harrigan" and "You're A Grand Old Flag".

1908

Old records show that the first attempt at operating passenger boat service between here and New York was made by the "Viva", in 1908. A yacht of 78 feet, the "Viva", was brought to the resort by a Captain Richard Dekyne and William Smith. The vessel was scheduled to run to New York daily from the Royal Palace Hotel, on Pacific Avenue at the Inlet, but on her very first voyage, June 6, 1908, she was wrecked on the Inlet sand bar. No casualties were reported.

Royal Palace Hotel and Casino
Atlantic City, N. J.

Made by Chilton Company, Philadelphia, Pa.

On the entertainment scene a vaudeville show, presented by Weis and Weinberger, at 1615 Boardwalk, was called "The Children's Delight and Old Folk's Paradise". Admission. believe it or not, was one cent!

The Victoria Theatre, on the Boardwalk near Arkansas Avenue, opened that year, showing movies only. Prior to that time, the Alhambra Theatre at Arkansas Avenue showed moving pictures a few nights a week, and sometimes for the entire week, depending on the season of the year. The Bijou Company opened a theatre at 1336 Atlantic Avenue, in 1908, and also showed movies. The Lyric Moving Picture Show, operated by Leo Weiler and Ira Parker, opened at 1806 Atlantic Avenue and continued in operation for many years. That same summer, Harry Brown and Harry Savage opened the Elite Theatre on Atlantic Avenue near Missouri, and the motion picture business in Atlantic City was off and running!

In those early days, people referred to the movies as "the flickers" and indeed with good reason! Projection and film equipment was far from perfect and the picture often jumped all over the screen! But the movies, even though they left much to be desired, were a big improvement over the lantern slides which had preceded them!

Barbershop quartets continued very popular and produced beautiful close harmony on such hits of the day as "Cuddle Up A Little Closer", "Shine On Harvest Moon", "I Wish I Had A Girl", "Take Me Out To The Ball Game" and "Every Day Is Ladies' Day With Me."

1909

The Venice Park Railroad was incorporated May 10, to lay track from the Shore Fast Line through Ohio Avenue to Grammercy Place. A single track closed car met Fast Line cars and carried passengers to a real estate development in Venice Park, which was then underway. Track was extended across the Penrose Canal to Central Avenue, now Kuehnle Avenue and Riverside Drive. A later extension was a connection with the Central Passenger Railway at Adriatic and South Carolina Avenues. Cars were operated from the Boardwalk over South Carolina Avenue to Venice Park. The West Jersey and Seashore retained the right to operate trains over the tracks of the trolley line with steam locomotives moving freight cars, usually at night, from the Inlet in Atlantic City down to Longport.

Atlantic City High School, Atlantic City, N. J.

I. & M. Ottenheimer, Balto., Maryland. Photo by H. B. Smith.

39

The class of '09 Atlantic City High School was, according to the local press, a record-breaker with 56 graduates at commencement exercises held in the Music Hall of Steel Pier. Harry Cassman was Class President. Very few extra police were hired that summer for a reason which sounds familiar today: a lack of funds! Sunday baseball was banned in our town and violation of the ordinance carried a fine of $200! Speaking of baseball, an electric scoreboard was installed on Young's Pier, on which American League games were reproduced in detail on a diamond. Fans could follow the plays on the board by watching the flashing electric lights.

Commuters were not too happy about a 10¢ increase in fare for the train between here and Philadelphia, bringing the cost for a Pullman seat to 35¢! Elsewhere on the transportation scene, the Atlantic City Electric Company was touting the electric car, and was inviting people to stop in for a demonstration ride. Two persons driving a Woods electric automobile set a new record for a trip on one battery charge: Philadelphia to Atlantic City and return, a distance of 134 3/10 miles, in three hours, 45 minutes! And a flagman at the Pennsylvania Reading Railroad crossing, in Absecon, recorded no less than 500 autos heading for Atlantic City on a Sunday that summer, between 9 A.M. and 5 P.M.!

Childs and Company, "with four stores on Atlantic Avenue at 801, 1613, 1931 and 2431", advertised a one-pound can of corned beef for 12¢, and a two-pound can for 20¢! Also "Parlor" matches, at three boxes for 10¢, and cider vinegar for 17¢ a gallon. If you enjoyed dining out on a limited budget, you paid a visit to Schoen's 15¢ Restaurant, Oyster Saloon and Ice Cream Parlor, at 12 South Mississippi, where you could enjoy "Meals at all hours: 15¢"!

Six-day bicycle races were being held on Young's Pier in 1909, and "Buffalo Bill's Wild West combined with Pawnee Bill's Far East Show" was booked for the Show Grounds on June 5. That was at Albany and Atlantic Avenues. Then, as now, we tried to lure conventions and a delegation of men from the American Order of Steam Engineers traveled to Reading, Pennsylvania, to the national convention to sell them the idea of holding their next conclave in Atlantic City.

In addition to the ban on Sunday baseball, there were two other campaigns being waged, one clamping down on unlicensed dogs on our streets and boardwalk, and another against slot machines! 190 liquor licenses were issued for the city that year. And, oh yes . . . post card vendors were being hauled into court to answer charges of selling cards showing women in scanty bathing attire, and the local paper carried a story which read in part, "It has been reported that several vendors in the fourth ward have been particularly bold in overstepping the bounds of decency".

Among the popular songs that year were "Meet Me Tonight In Dreamland", "Put On Your Old Grey Bonnet", "I've Got Rings On My Fingers" (Bells On My Toes), "My Hero" and "I Wonder Who's Kissing Her Now", composed by Joe E. Howard, who spent many a summer here.

1910

Walter Wellman, a polar explorer, took off from Atlantic City that year in a dirigible named "America", in an early attempt at a transoceanic flight. Wellman and his brave crew traveled 375 miles out to sea before the airship became unmanageable and had to be abandoned. They were rescued by a passing steamship off Cape Hatteras, North Carolina. The engine in Wellman's craft had seen previous service in an automobile, so perhaps that had something to do with the failure of the venture!

The George A. McKeague Co., Specialists in Photography, No. 43 Law Bldg., Atlantic City, N. J.

For those of you who have never experienced the thrill of seeing one of those silent titans of the skies, a dirigible was a rigid, lighter-than-aircraft, filled with helium and shaped like a huge cigar which carried passengers in surprising comfort, after it was further developed. Wellman's airship was not as sophisticated as later dirigibles, but it marked a milestone in the history of air transportation.

Walter Brookins, a protege of the famous Wright brothers, flew a Wright "aeroplane", the name by which they were known at that time, over the resort, establishing a world's record while reaching the incredible altitude of 5800 feet! The Air Carnival that year, held under the auspices of the local Aero Club, saw Glenn Curtiss make a flight of 50 miles back and forth over the ocean in one hour, 14 minutes, in a "pusher" type plane, dropping oranges on an anchored yacht to demonstrate the bombing potential of aircraft in time of war!

Rail transportation in 1910 was very dependable and, according to the timetable for "The Reading", the summer of that year saw 17 trains daily running between Atlantic City and Philadelphia! The local station was at Arkansas and Atlantic Avenues. A one-dollar excursion from the Quaker City to the foot of Mississippi Avenue here, departed at 7 A.M. arriving in Atlantic City at 8:30! Not bad time at all! In addition, there were

W. G. Mac Farlane, Publisher & Importer. Printed in Germany.

fast express trains roaring along the rails between here and New York, via Lakewood. One left Manhattan at 10 A.M. and arrived at the shore at 1:10 P.M. There were comfortable Pullman parlor cars on all express trains. Most stopped at Massachusetts, Delaware, Virginia, South Carolina and Kentucky Avenues. A. D. Tice was General Manager of the local station with Edson J. Weeks the Passenger Agent, and W. H. McCormick serving as Assistant Passenger Agent.

Entire households followed the "funnies" or comic strips and laughed at the antics of "Little Nemo" and "The Yellow Kid." In March, City Council adopted an ordinance providing for the purchase of Albany Avenue Park, at an estimated cost of $175,000.

A passenger and freight vessel, the "Brazoria", ran aground on a sandbar off the Royal Palace Hotel in the Inlet, in August, in heavy seas. Waves smashed her stern port and with a rising tide, the craft drifted onto the north bar finally breaking up amidships. Her cargo was salvaged and all passengers and crew got off without incident. Four days later, a violent storm finished her off and she was listed as a total loss by her owners.

1911

One of the places to visit when you came to Atlantic City, in 1911 was Captain John Young's spectacular Million Dollar Pier, stretching out to sea from the Boardwalk at Arkansas Avenue! Joseph Dawson was Booking Agent and Director of Carnivals for the big amusement center, and what attractions it offered! From an old program, we quote some of the flowery descriptions of its many features: "The Hippodrome Theatre with thrillers culled from the circuits . . . A departure from vaudeville with daring aerialists, gymnasts, daredevil tumblers, trained animals and

No Publisher listed.

circus clowns, performing daily at 3:15 and 8:15 P.M.". Then there were the unique net hauls, described in the brochure as "a roundup of deep sea denizens, tons of finny spoil in a single hauling . . . The rarest of shore sights". I recall seeing hundreds of fish of all sizes and many species, flopping around in that net as it was pulled from the bottom of the ocean,alongside the pier. Some were sold for food, while many found their way into the pier's big aquariums, due to their rarity.

Dawson's Dancing Dolls and Children's Carnival was a major attraction Monday, Wednesday and Friday evenings, with the "Grand March" at 8 o'clock! Joe Hortiz' Minstrel Boys, a mainstay of the famous Dumont's Minstrels, put on an elaborate production which really packed 'em in! Remember those interlocutors and "Mr. Bones" ?? And, of course, your visit to the pier wasn't complete without a tour of Captain Young's famous cottage, described here earlier.

That home, "#1 Atlantic Ocean", had many important visitors, including President William Howard Taft, who was a guest in 1911. The President marvelled at the ornate furniture and statuary, as well as its beautiful garden with an arbor covered with imitation grapes, which looked just like the real thing! The Chief Executive was in town to address the Christian Endeavor Convention. In 1911, the population of our city was 46,150 and growing all the time!

Some of the tunes most likely on the lips of localites were, "Ah, Sweet Mystery of Life", "Alexander's Ragtime Band", "I Want A Girl Just Like The Girl", (Who Married Dear Old Dad), "Somewhere A Voice Is Calling" and "Oh, You Beautiful Doll".

The first airplane license in Atlantic City, for passenger flights, was issued in June to the aforementioned Glenn H. Curtiss. For many years thereafter, Curtiss operated aircraft out of the Inlet, taking many

43

people for their first flight, in the wild blue yonder, in the skies over Atlantic City.

The real estate business was enjoying great success and the Venice Park development was sold to Louis Kuehnle and George F. Joly, Jr. Venice Park, just off Absecon Boulevard near Ohio Avenue, covers approximately 40 acres and was originally planned to feature canals, much the same as Venice, Italy, hence its name.

And our city mourned the passing of Mayor Franklin P. Stoy, who had helped guide the destinies of the resort since 1900. Mayor Stoy died while in office on July 22nd, 1911.

Published by Saltzburg's Merchandise Co., Atlantic City, N. J.

1912

Old-timers still talk of the "Tornado of 1912", here in Atlantic City. What was described officially as the tail of a tornado, swept down from Lake Erie on Sunday, July 21, smashing into the resort at about 6 p.m. It rode along on a thunderstorm and for two harrowing hours caused great damage to property, with thousands of people on our beaches and boardwalk being caught with little or no warning! This was before the weather bureau had the expertise it has today. So far as we can learn, there was no loss of life attributed to the storm but trees and signboards were brought down, windows were broken and vehicles damaged.

1912 also saw the first locally-owned commercial gasoline vehicle, in our town. It belonged to a produce vendor, Andrew Schlachter. In those days, hucksters traveled around the city following regular routes dispensing their fruits and vegetables door-to-door. Atlantic City boasted 1,000 hotels, large and small and more than 5,000 guest houses, and to handle the resulting business, we had eight banks! They were Marine Trust, Second National, Atlantic City Deposit and Trust, Union National, Guarantee Trust Company, Chelsea National, Boardwalk National and First National. Again, we had two Mayors during that year. Harry Bacharach and William Riddle.

The Spearman Pub. Company, Atlantic City, N. J.

The original Young's Pier, Tennessee Avenue and the Beach, was the scene of a disastrous fire on March 29th. It was not destroyed, however, and stands today as Central Pier. The old pier enjoyed fame as the home of the cakewalk, a dance craze of the period, and was known as "Young's Old Pier" following construction of the Million Dollar Pier, in 1906. After the fire of 1912, the pier lay in ruins for years until its purchase by the city as a possible Convention Hall site. In 1922, it was rebuilt by the Central Pier Company and has been used for offices, amusements and exhibits, including an aquarium, since that time.

The Y.M.C.A. building on Pacific Avenue was dedicated that July and a man who was elected to the Presidency of the United States that year, did the honors. He was New Jersey Governor Woodrow Wilson, who became our Chief Executive the following November.

And around the city one could hear such songs as "Be My Little Baby Bumble Bee", "It's A Long Way To Tipperary", "My Melancholy Baby", "Waiting For The Robert E. Lee", and "Moonlight Bay."

1913

Moving pictures with sound were first shown in the resort during the season of 1913. They were produced by the synchronization of a phonograph record with the reel of the film, an invention of New Jersey's own Thomas A. Edison. Grand Opera was among the many screen offerings including "The Temptation of Faust" and "Julius Caesar" with a new show weekly. And which movie house showed those early "Talkies"? It was the Savoy.

Believe it or not, we had a newsreel of sorts in those days called

45

"Atlantic City Weekly". Newsreels were popular until just after World War II, bringing audiences in theatres the news very much as we see it today on television. What was contained in that early newsreel is not documented since none has been located in any local archives, but it reportedly did stories on runaway teams of horses, bicycle riding "scorchers", auto "joy riders", visits of important people and political happenings. Regular motion pictures which "talked" still were about 15 years in the future.

A new idea took form when the possibilities of laying a salt water main along the oceanfront were being discussed, but the cost turned out to be prohibitive. Ocean water cannot be pumped for fire fighting use unless it is taken from deep water, since sand drawn up with the water results in damage to the equipment. The Mayor of Atlantic City at that time was William Riddle who served until 1916.

The highest temperature ever recorded in Atlantic City was on August 7, 1913, when the mercury soared to 104 degrees! Carrol Brown, of Atlantic City, helped pitch the old Philadelphia Athletics baseball team to the American League Championship that year with a victory over the New York Giants, in the World Series! The Guarantee Bank Building on Atlantic Avenue near Pennsylvania, was purchased by the bank in 1913. It had been erected in 1903, and was then known as the Bartlett Building. Today, it houses the headquarters of the Siracusa Company.

Song-pluggers in music stores on the avenue and the boardwalk and in beer gardens around town featured such popular ditties as "Danny Boy", "If I Had My Way", "You Made Me Love You", "Peg O' My Heart" and "When Irish Eyes Are Smiling."

1914

1914 was another happy year around the nation, and millions of visitors converged on Atlantic City that innocent, carefree summer! A contest was conducted by our Chamber of Commerce to find a good slogan for the city. The winner was Leon F. Rubens, who designed the famous Atlantic City "Clock" sign with the slogan "Atlantic City All The Time". It isn't seen very much anymore, but now that we have become a 12-months-a-year resort, it might be a good idea to dust it off! As the winner, Mr. Rubens received the handsome sum of $25 for his work, which was officially adopted by the city in March of 1914. In the center of the clock were the words "All The Time". In the first circle, "Atlantic City" appeared where the numerals normally are. The outer circle was marked by the months, indicating ours was a year-'round resort. Made into a large electric sign, it was on display in front of City Hall, on Atlantic Avenue, during the big carnival that year, and was used in many forms of advertising, including printed matter, for many years.

The Chamber of Commerce was incorporated in 1914 and had as its first President Joseph A. McNamee, who succeeded Joseph W. Salus as President of the old City Business League, the forerunner of the Chamber. A permanent staff of ten persons was employed.

From a brochure put out by "The Reading", in 1914, we get a good

Visitors to Atlantic City stroll the Boardwalk in 1914

idea of what Atlantic City was like then. The publication touted the city as "The premier pleasure and health resort of America with only a few European resorts rivaling it for year-'round enjoyment". Superior train service enabled local residents to commute to Philadelphia and New York daily to conduct their businesses, and many families moved to the shore for the summer with the breadwinner taking the train to and from his work, happy to be able to enjoy the cool comfort here and to know his family was having a nice vacation! G. B. Kaufman was the line's Passenger Agent, with his office at North Carolina Avenue and the Boardwalk.

A 1914 ad in my collection of advertising memorabilia shows gorgeous dolls for little girls priced from 98¢ all the way up to $4.95 . . . collector's items today! For boys, there were those wonderful Erector sets priced from 89¢ to $8.99.

The player piano was a popular piece of furniture in many local homes and among the tunes on those paper rolls were, "Down Among The Sheltering Palms", "12th Street Rag", "When You're Away", "Can't You Hear Me Calling, Caroline?" and "There's A Long, Long Trail".

Pub. by P. Sander, Philadelphia and Atlantic City.

1915

After years of public transportation in the form of horse-drawn trolleys, followed by electric ones, Atlantic City saw the inauguration of jitney service in March of 1915. These were simply passenger automobiles, used to carry the public to and fro. The service was first established on Atlantic Avenue, with the "fleet" made up of two open touring cars operating at a fare of five cents. The name "jitney" came about because that was then the slang term for a nickel! The name stuck and today, those "buslets" running the length of Pacific Avenue, still are known as jitneys, although the old original 5-cent fare is long forgotten. Each is privately owned and maintained.

Atlantic City jitney, possibly a 1930 Cadillac. Note front-seat passenger. Fred Hess Photo from the collection of Jeffrey Marinoff.

It is hard to believe, but by year's end, more than 400 private vehicles of every description and vintage were traveling Atlantic Avenue. They gave irregular service; wherever the last passenger got off was the end of the line. I remember jitneys in the 30's and 40's when big, old seven-passenger sedans and limousines still were in use, mainly Cadillacs, Packards, Pierce-Arrows, Buicks and Lincolns. Many of them were equipped with a rope rigged so the driver could release the handle of the rear door and we could get out. And many's the time I rode up front with the driver!

Jitney service proved so popular with the public that first year that it cut into trolley income and a receiver was appointed for the Atlantic City and Shore Railroad.

On the local entertainment scene, the Apollo Theatre on the Boardwalk near New York Avenue, featured what was advertised as "Elite Vaudeville, with a diversified program".

One of their handbills that year advertised "Bounding Johnson" on the High-Wire; Hazel Moran and Miss Mae Peck, Comedienne, and "Klaw and Erlanger's Entertainers". Later that season, the Apollo featured a Keystone Comedy, "The Newman Travel Talks", described as "Exquisite Color Views with E. M. Newman, Noted Traveler and Lecturer". In 1915, the Eastern Motor Company, 2207 Atlantic Avenue, was selling the new Hudson cars for $1,550. Local druggists were advertising "Fast Step" foot powder as a remedy for "Boardwalk Feet", a complaint by visitors not used to walking the wooden planks for hours!

Atlantic City hotels catered to people from every walk of life and you were certain to find one which suited your pocketbook from among the Arcadia, Austine, Galen Hall, Elberon, Royal Palace, Rudolf, Vendig and Warwick, to name a few.

Hotel Rudolf, Atlantic City, N. J.

The Chas. H. Elliott Co., North Philadelphia.

49

Folks were learning the words to some of the new songs of the day, including "Memories", "Are You From Dixie?", "She's The Daughter of Mother Machree", "The Sunshine Of Your Smile" and "There's A Broken Heart For Every Light On Broadway".

1916

This is the year the Breakers Hotel, formerly the Rudolf, was re-opened and dedicated, along with the new St. Charles, at a huge banquet at the Breakers, which stood on the Boardwalk at New Jersey Avenue, opposite Garden Pier. The St. Charles was destroyed by fire in 1952, while the Breakers met its end at the hands of demolition experts using dynamite, in 1974.

The city purchased four mechanized chemical and hose combination wagons for the Fire Department, which eventually sent all our fire horses to pasture! There were 59 applications for liquor licenses bringing the total in the city to 121! One could buy a beautiful "Grafanola" phonograph for $85 in local stores. City commission okayed the use of a powerful searchlight to make night bathing possible for day workers who couldn't visit the beach at normal times.

In that year before America went to war, a three-room house in Margate at Ventnor and Madison Avenues rented for $75 . . . for the season! And one could rent a store on Pacific Avenue for $200 a year.

The first local man to leave for the Mexican border crisis to fight Pancho Villa was Frank M. Beckett, a fireman from the Tennessee Avenue station. Professor Henry Miller was the principal at Atlantic City High School, then located at Ohio and Pacific Avenues, and the graduating class that year numbered 118!

Lumitone Photoprint, New York.

All-night trolley service in the city was restored on an hourly schedule. Jitney drivers were now required to turn over 3% of their gross earnings to the city. Three were delinquent and the city brought suit to collect! The Gulf Service Station, still located at Albany and Ventnor Avenues, near the monument, opened on June 26.

And a Military Instructor was hired by our Police Department. He was Drillmaster Charles Beach, who announced when he was hired, that the men under his command would drill just like soldiers! And Beach saw to it that all automobile laws in the city were strictly enforced.

For those who enjoyed a little nip now and then, Abe Freeman Cut Price Liquors, 1516 Atlantic Avenue, featured specials which today are almost unbelievable! For example: one quart of "Three Queens Whisky" and one quart of Holland Gin, complete with a suitcase in which to carry it, plus a glass and a corkscrew, all for the amazing price of $1.75! And how about this at Freeman's: one quart Sherry Wine and one quart Manhattan or Martini cocktails, along with a case in which to carry it, for $1.50! "Penn" Beer sold for a dollar for a 24-bottle case.

THE BOARDWALK AND HOTELS DUNLOP, CHALFONTE AND STRAND, ATLANTIC CITY, N. J.

The Union News Company.

Tennis was a popular sport 'way back then at the Yacht Club Courts. And the Vandal A. C. defeated the Atlantic City Cyclones 10-6 at Bacharach Park. The city's Aquatic Club's water polo team used the pool at the Brighton Casino and was practicing to meet the Melrose A. C.

In show business, there was always something for everyone, as the saying goes, on stage, screen and cabaret, as well as at the hotels and piers. Nixon's Apollo was featuring David Belasco presenting Frances Starr in "Little Lady In Blue"; The Hotel Dunlop, on the Boardwalk at Ocean Avenue starred Peggy Kavanaugh and the Palm Beach Troubadours. There were tango contests on The Million Dollar Pier and Singer's Midgets were at Nixon's. On the silver screen, silent movies drew hundreds to each performance to view such thrill-packed fare as, "The Ordeal of Elizabeth" at the City Square, Tennessee and Atlantic;

"The Fireman", starring Charlie Chaplin at the Bijou and "The Closed Road", with House Peters, at the Anita, Boardwalk at Florida Avenue.

Many veterans of the Civil War were living at that time and the Department of New Jersey's Grand Army of the Republic held its encampment here, in June. Five beachfront hotels got the local Y.M.C.A. off to a good start with donations of $5,000 each to help pay off the Y's debts. The goal was $75,000.

If you were living here or visiting, you probably stopped in at Stadler's Ice Cream and Cherry Pie Store, 10 S. Virginia Avenue, Brigadell's Cut Price Drug Store, Montpelier and Atlantic, and Major's Drug Store, Indiana and Atlantic. Patriotism was running high in 1916 and Hurley-Jones Department Store was selling four-by-six foot American flags for 85¢!

1916 saw the second City Commission election in May with voters balloting directly for five Commissioners by choice. That is, each person expressed first, second, third and so on, while they were in the booth. The five men receiving the highest number of first choice votes were elected. There were 25 candidates in that May 9th election. When it was over and the paper ballots were tallied, the winners were Harry Bacharach, Albert Beyer, W. Frank Sooy, Charles D. White and Dr. Jesse B. Thompson.

GIANT UNDERWOOD TYPEWRITER, UNDERWOOD GARDEN PIER EXHIBIT, ATLANTIC CITY, N. J.

Published by Saltzburg's Merchandise Co., Atlantic City, N. J.

A giant Underwood typewriter arrived in the resort, in 1916, from the Panama-Pacific Exposition in San Francisco and thrilled millions for more than 20 years as it stood on exhibit at Garden Pier and in the auditorium. I didn't see it until 1930, and what an experience that was! I sent my mom and dad this post card showing the huge machine. It was activated by a standard-size typewriter, and was eventually dismantled during World War II, after being exhibited at the New York World's Fair in 1939.

Getting back to 1916, some of the year's best songs were "I'm Sorry I Made You Cry", "Nola", "Pretty Baby", "Poor Butterfly" and "Turn Back The Universe And Give Me Yesterday".

Hotels Islesworth and Scarborough, Atlantic City, N. J.

No Publisher listed.

1917

Homes throughout the city displayed a star in the window, signifying that a son, husband or father had gone to war . . . the "war to end all wars"! Atlantic County stood seventh in the state in total number of enlistments and all males between the ages of 15 and 50 were being urged to enlist in the home guard. The black community formed two full companies with Benjamin Fitzgerald and Joseph Ford as prime movers. To keep up spirits, people jammed local entertainment emporiums to sing, dance and try to escape, if only for a fleeting moment or two, the shadow of war. Sophie Tucker was appearing, in person, at the Hotel Islesworth Rose Gardens on Virginia Avenue. The Hotel Dunlap's cabaret was featuring May Mills in "Seashore Frolics" and the Inlet Pavilion opened that July with a girl billed as "Atlantic City's Favorite Songbird", Viola Sheehey!

A move to place a woman on the Atlantic City Board of Education was begun by Mrs. Arthur Chenoweth, who planned to petition the panel to consider the nomination of Mrs. Warren Somers. Patriotism was running high and there was no problem getting some two-thousand persons to form a human flag on the beach between Tennessee and South Carolina Avenues, that Fourth of July! It must have been something to see from an upper floor of a boardwalk hotel! Incidentally, that holiday saw a throng of some 200,000 in the city with train after train departing just as soon as they were loaded!

Baseball was a very popular sport in those days and competion was keen among various neighborhood teams. Two of them, the Bacharach Giants and the Logan Square boys played an 18-inning, one-to-one tie game that summer. Cowboy boxing champion Jess Willard came to town, in person, and appeared at the Inlet ball park as a feature of the Buffalo Bill Wild West Show.

An old friend of mine, the late William "Whitey" Thomas, was bitten by a dog on the beach, causing Mayor Harry Bacharach to institute a law banning all canines from that area. Thomas joined the Army Air Corps and flew the famous "Spad" aeroplanes in World War I, in France. He was a member of the Atlantic City Beach Patrol both before and after his war service.

An ad in "The Atlantic City Press" was looking for "A chauffeur experienced in driving and repairing the Packard car". The new Chalmers touring was selling for $1,200 at the showroom of W. J. Houpt, 311 Atlantic Avenue, while George Mason was the Overland distributor at California and Atlantic. Frank P. Gravatt, who would later become the owner of Steel Pier as well as the operator of several hotels in the city, was the agent for the Iver-Johnson, Pierce and Reading Standard bicycles and you could buy one for as little as a dollar a week!

At the movies, people enjoyed Rex Beach's "The Barrier" at The Criterion; Jules Verne's "20,000 Leagues Under The Sea" at the Nixon; "Poor Little Rich Girl" starring Mary Pickford, at the Bijou; The Steel Pier was advertising Vesella and His Italian Band, Cake Walk Contests, Murphy's American Minstrels, and a Children's Carnival. Young's Million Dollar Pier offered Dawson's Dancing Dolls, a Tango Contest and the famous Emmet Welch's Minstrels in the huge Hippodrome Theatre.

The tax rate in our city that year was $2.30 and the Commissioners were saying they hoped to hold the line but thought it might go up.

Some of 1917's hit songs were "Give Me The Moonlight, Give Me The Girl", "Oh Johnny, Oh", "Roses Of Picardy", "Over There" and "For Me And My Gal".

1918

The big new of 1918 was, of course, the signing of the Armistice on November 11, officially ending hostilities between Germany and the United States in the great war before we had assigned them numbers. Pandemonium reigned all around the city when the news broke, with whistles, horns, firecrackers and guns joining all kinds of makeshift noise-makers celebrating the arrival of peace! Very few people slept as the big party continued!

Earlier in the year, on June 4, a lifeboat arrived on the South Carolina Avenue beach carrying 28 survivors of a torpedoed steamship, the "Carolina". They had rowed for some 40 hours following the sinking of their vessel. Among them were eight women and two children.

A bill was introduced in City Commission to abolish the practice of providing free lunches at saloons to boost the sale of liquor. And a new ordinance required the ice man to place cake weighing 50 pounds or more in the box, while cakes under that size were to be left in receptacles placed outside the entrance to the building! 18 members of the Electrical Linemen's Union went on strike asking a boost in pay from 60¢ an hour to 75¢. They were given a 10¢ increase! And the trolley strikes ended, with the employees now receiving as much as 35¢ an hour and a 10-hour day instead of the former 12.

The Traymore Hotel management bought an ad in the Daily Press vowing to use no wheat flour til the new crop was in, so that our fighting men in France would have an ample supply for bread! The Chalfonte Hotel bought an adjoining lot, with a 90-foot front, for $40,000. A Milwaukee businessman, George Bartlett, was staying at the Chalfonte and suggested the possiblity of laying concrete for a highway connecting Atlantic City with Camden.

Floodlights were again installed for night bathing at the Virginia and South Carolina Avenue beaches, an innovation which had been introduced two years earlier and proved most popular. A local pastor was lamenting the lack of parental guidance for our young people, especially girls, who were congregating at late hours in public parks!

Completion of a high pressure water system from Maine to Morris Avenues now permitted 150-pounds of pressure in the event of fire along our boardwalk. Eight hotels had joined forces in the project, headed by Albert Bell of the Chalfonte-Haddon Hall, to supply pressure from their own pumps which boosted the supply of 12,000 gallons per minute from the city mains to 150 pounds per square inch, giving fire engine pressure at the moment of alarm! Members of that group were the St. Charles, Galen Hall, Breakers, Traymore, Chalfonte-Haddon Hall, Brighton, Marlborough-Blenheim and Dennis Hotels.

Pub. by Koffman Bros., Atlantic City, N. J.

The Adams Express Company was handling baggage and express to Longport from Atlantic City, cargo which had been brought to the resort by train. One "combine" street car carried newspapers and mail to Longport and one was assigned to the Venice Park Line. Another wartime change was the conversion of two open cars as "center entrance" cars. These, along with others, were used mostly during evening hours, from the Boardwalk at Virginia Avenue to the Savannah Avenue loop in Margate.

Walking the boards always has whipped up an appetite for most people and in 1918, one could buy delicious "red hots" or hot dogs for 5¢ and wash 'em down with refreshing root beer or orange ade for another nickel!

"Live" shows were the rage and Keith's Garden Pier, on the Boardwalk at New Jersey Avenue was showing "Maytime", with John Charles Thomas, while the Apollo featured "Hitchy Koo: 1918" with Leon Errol and Irene Bordoni. The Moulin Rouge, Boardwalk at New York Avenue was proud of its "Girlie Revue".

Abe Freeman, 1516 Atlantic Avenue who has been mentioned earlier for his great discount prices on spirits, also sold cigarettes at big savings, advertising Piedmont, Oasis and Sweet Caporals at 9¢ a pack; Murads and Melachrinos at 16¢; Chesterfields and Lucky Strikes were two packs for 27¢, while Helmar 100's sold for $1.10 per package!

War songs were popular in 1918 and after, and here are just a few: "Hello Central, Give Me No Man's Land", "Good Morning, Mr. Zip Zip Zip", "Just A Baby's Prayer At Twilight", "Oh, How I Hate To Get Up In The Morning" and "The Rose Of No Man's Land".

1919

Even then, people were air-minded and Atlantic City was selected as the site for the Pan-American Aeronautical Congress, which convened on Steel Pier, that May. Many flyers, just back from the war, welcomed the opportunity to pilot aircraft in peaceful skies. Among the many events scheduled were various aerial gymnastics orginating at the newly opened Atlantic City Airport.

Among the incentives to attract participants was a $500 prize for the first flyer to land in the city. According to old records, it went to a Lieutenant who flew his small plane from New York in two hours, 10 minutes. A highlight of the air show was the dropping of a crate of eggs by parachute. None were broken! They were later sold as souvenirs at a quarter each!

The word "airport" reportedly was coined in Atlantic City by Henry Woodhouse who reasoned that this was a wonderful place for a seaport so why not an "Air-Port"? The facility, located within the city limits, was later re-named Bader Field in honor of Mayor Edward L. Bader and was managed by Bevan "Bev" Baldwin who was called from Franklin Field in Philadelphia to come here and lend his expertise in the building of an athletic field. The project eventually wound up as an athletic field and an airport.

The price of the "Daily Press" went up to 2¢ in 1919. High cost of labor and materials was cited. It was one of the last of the nation's dailies to boost its price to 2¢! Teachers in the city were complaining about their low salaries with a pay range of $750 to $1,300 annually. But we still were ahead of Trenton with its $700 minimum and $1,000 maximum!

The Parkway Apartments, Boston and Atlantic Avenues, was on the market for $110,000! A crackdown on the sale of hard liquor went into effect by order of the Department of Justice, and even though it was after the war, it was referred to as "Wartime Prohibition". Within a few days most beachfront cafes and many saloons had removed whiskey and gin from their premises.

The Victory Market, 929 Atlantic Avenue was selling breast of lamb for 13¢ a pound; prime rib roast was 38¢ and picnic hams were going for 30¢ a pound!

A new record was set for July 4, when 45,000 persons visited our city for the big holiday! And local entertainment spots where music was featured, and that was just about everywhere, presented such lilting melodies as "Alice Blue Gown", "Dardanella", "Indian Summer", "Let The Rest Of The World Go By", and "A Pretty Girl Is Like A Melody".

1920

Mayor Bader was urging a ban on slowly-moving traffic on Pacific Avenue to speed things up with the possibility of eventually making it a one-way street! Sound familiar? And this was 60 years ago! His Honor remarked in the local press that, "It was worth your life to try to cross Pacific Avenue on foot" and said he'd never seen so many autos in town as he saw that summer!

Speaking of autos, C.H.K. Motor Company, 2720 Atlantic Avenue, was agent for the Cole Aero Eight, while Walden's, at Providence and Atlantic, was showing the latest model Clevelands!

The men who pushed our rolling chairs along the boardwalk went on strike for more money, demanding 50¢ an hour for chairs with two persons and 75¢ an hour for those carrying three! Cabaret fees in the city were raised to $150 a year, and Judge John White objected to a request by their owners to extend the 1 A.M. curfew, saying it would play into the hands of the underworld and would foster crime.

The free employment bureau of the Chamber of Commerce placed 761 persons in jobs that June. And the first American Legion post for women veterans of the great war to be chartered in our state, was organized here in 1920!

A truckload of illicit liquor was confiscated in a garage on Arkansas Avenue, as a group of men tried to sell 46 cases of the stuff! $50,000 was pledged in eight minutes at the Breakers Hotel at a meeting on behalf of a bond issue for the Linwood Country Club, in the amount of $100,000!

Air service between the resort and New York loomed as a reality with the hopes that a regular passenger route could be established. In July, a dozen planes of various types flew into town. The center of attention were an Aeromarine Navy Cruiser, a kind of flying boat, and the Curtiss Flying Fish. Each carried between 14 and 16 passengers. The Atlantic City Aero Club and The Hotelmen's Association teamed up to provide the impetus required to get the thing off the ground, as it were! Fare was set at $75 each way between here and New York.

Atlantic City Electric filed for a revised schedule of rates that summer, in which it asked for a boost to 12¢ per kilowatt hour for the first 30 KW; 11¢ for the next 30 KW and 10¢ for all above 60!

City Hall employees were imploring the commission for Saturdays off "for those who could be spared". They all were working a half day on Saturdays, year 'round, and it appeared they would continue to do so, since their request did not fall on compassionate ears.

Songs? You bet 1920 had 'em! And they're heard today, they were that good: "I'll Be With You In Apple Blossom Time", "Margie", "Avalon", "Whispering" and "When My Baby Smiles At Me".

The staff at the "Press" got a big surprise when, in July of that year, they had a visitor named J. R. Edmiston, of Charleston, South Carolina and Baltimore, Maryland. Edmiston claimed it was he who "invented" salt water taffy in 1884, when his little taffy stand, between the Boardwalk and the Victoria Skating Rink on South Carolina Avenue, had been wet down overnight by a heavy surf. Next morning, he invited his first customer to enjoy some "salt water taffy", and the rest is history. In 1920, Edmiston, then in his 80's, was in town to renew old acquaintance with his friend of earlier days, Captain John Young.

By 1920, we could boast a population of 50,682!

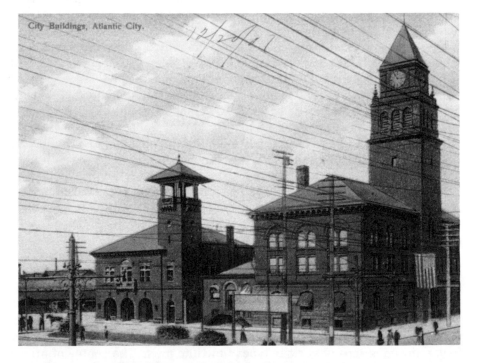

Osograph. Osborne Ltd., 22 E. 21st St., New York (Germany).

1921

If you were living in Atlantic City in '21 and were at least seven or eight years old, you probably recall the good times you had at Rendezvous Park, which opened in May. Rendezvous Park was short-lived, however, being torn down a few years later to make way for our new Convention Hall. It was a huge amusement center taking in the entire block bounded by the Boardwalk, and Mississippi, Georgia and Pacific Avenues! Rendezvous Park boasted a dance floor which could accommodate 2000 dancing couples! And there was a bath house, restaurants, and amusements galore, including the popular shoot-the-shoot or roller coaster. Records show that the park was illuminated by some 30,000 electric lights! The original cost of Rendezvous Park? Three-million 1921 dollars!

This was the year Atlantic City went on Daylight Saving time. And a Margate resident, Casner S. Risley, made history when, with his homemade amateur radio equipment, was heard across the Atlantic Ocean seven times within a 10-day period! The local press, at that time, commented: "Risley has reflected great honor upon his native city, and has made both his name and that of his city known on both sides of the Atlantic." Risley had begun his early experiments with a crystal detector set at the age of 12. His official call was 3BGT.

Some of the year's more popular tunes were "I'm Just Wild About Harry" written by the legendary Eubie Blake; "Ma, He's Making Eyes At Me"; "Second Hand Rose", "Peggy O'Neill" and "The Sheik Of Araby".

The city had a 30-piece Fireman's Band then, of which it was most proud. Band Director was Frank Merrick. City population was almost 51,000.

At local movie houses, D. W. Griffiths' "Way Down East", at the Globe, "The Love Chef", with Leo Carillo, at the Woods; "Land of Hope", with Alice Brady, at the Bijou, and at Nixon's Apollo: "The 15th Annual Ziegfeld Follies"!

The famed Ritz Carlton Hotel, on the Boardwalk at Iowa Avenue, opened that year amid much fanfare. The Ritz is where Enoch L. "Nucky" Johnson held forth while one of the most powerful political bosses Atlantic City has ever known! It is said that Nucky's parties at the Ritz were just fabulous and were often compared with anything to be found in New York or Hollywood! The original cost to build the Ritz Carlton was six million dollars. During World War II, it served as one of a number of local barracks for servicemen in training, as hotels were taken over by Uncle Sam for that purpose, "for the duration". In 1969, the Ritz was converted to apartments, and is now owned by a group of investors with plans to convert it again . . . this time into a multi-million dollar casino hotel complex.

The Ambassador Hotel opened its fabulous "Summer Garden", in June, and various "Nights", such as Egyptian, Hawaiian and Venetian Night, were featured! Other popular entertainment spots were Friar's Inn, Boardwalk at New York Avenue, and Moulin Rouge, on the opposite corner.

The Pageant Committee decided in 1921, to let the public select the man and woman who would play the roles of "Neptune" and "Neptuna"

340—Hotel Ambassador and Ritz Carlton, Atlantic City, N. J.

No Publisher listed.

in the big Fall Frolic, September 7th and 8th. And Mayor Bader stated that "nothing daring would be permitted" at the event. A local inventor claimed he had plans for a four mile-a-minute train to the shore from Philadelphia, utilizing the monorail concept. Imagine! Only 18 minutes between the two cities!

City fathers hired women "Copettes" to stroll our beaches watching for flirts, mashers and what were called "Beach Lizards", who tried to pick up young ladies! 28 members of the A.C.H.S. baseball squad left on the 7 A.M. Reading Express one morning for Philadelphia, to take on Girard College. Team captain was Bob Durham.

1922

Is it possible that Atlantic City had a condominium back in 1922? There was advertising that year calling attention to the fact that the Roxbury Apartments, 187 States Avenue, was available for tenant ownership of apartments. Plans called for a seven story building with six apartments on each floor.

Rum runners kept the federal agents busy trying to intercept small boats being used to bring ashore illicit booze from schooners from the West Indies, anchored offshore! The situation was serious enough to bring United States District Attorney Frederick W. Pearse to town to personally direct operations against the practice! Many were the local cafe owners, bartenders and waiters who were held on bail for their alleged participation in the shady business!

The Atlantic City Daily Press was putting out four editions: morning, noon, afternoon and night, at 2¢ per copy! Atlantic Citians were buying their Buicks from Hall and Gravatt, 2200 Atlantic Avenue. A beautiful sport touring model could be yours for only $1,785! Rickenbackers were sold at 107 N. Arkansas Avenue, while your area Hupmobile

Agency was Alex H. Latta, 1127 Baltic Avenue.

Mrs. Booker T. Washington, widow of the famous scientist and founder of Tuskegee Institute, spoke at Price Memorial A.M.E. Church that year. And F. Freeman Parker piloted his catboat "Stingaree" to victory for the Atlantic City Yacht Club, while a big Marathon Relay Race from Philadelphia to Atlantic City, in August, attracted more than 100 runners!

On the boardwalk, the Globe Theatre was featuring the team of Van and Schenck, Ona Munson and Patricola of the famous B.F. Keith Circuit, plus the vivacious French singer-comedienne, Fritzi Scheff! Million Dollar Pier offered dancing in their beautiful ballroom to the music of the Benson Orchestra of Chicago, and a big attraction was the Tango Contest with a prize of $75!

In July, the airport at Bader Field was purchased by the city. It had been privately owned before that. The deal included the land for an athletic field which was named for the man who was then our Mayor, Edward L. Bader. This fine facility is one of the few airports in the nation which is so close to the downtown section of the city, making it a popular landing site for owners of private planes flying in for conventions and on business. It cannot be enlarged, however, since it is bordered by the Inland Waterway and Albany Avenue Boulevard, a heavily traveled artery linking the resort with the mainland.

Our Police Accident Bureau opened in January. The growing number of motor vehicles caused an increasing number of accidents, hence the need for this new department which operated out of Police Headquarters. Today, it is part of the Traffic Bureau. The Harding Highway received its name as.a result of the visit in 1922, of President Warren G. Harding, to the home of Senator Walter E. Edge.

At the local A&P Store, one could buy eggs for 37¢ a dozen; five pounds of sugar for 34¢; Bokar coffee for 35¢ a pound, and if one chose to dine out, there was a great six-course meal served at the Garden Grille, 151 South New York Avenue for only 80¢! At the movies, folks enjoyed Jack Holt in "When Satan Sleeps", Wallace Reid in "The Dictator", Agnes Ayres in "The Ordeal" with Conrad Nagel, and Conway Tearle in "Love's Masquarade".

1923

The "monument in the middle of the street" at Albany and Ventnor Avenues, which has been both cursed and praised, was erected in 1923, and dedicated to Atlantic Citians who had fought in the World War. When it was originally planned, in 1907, the monument was to be merely decorative since war was far from the minds of the people, at that time. The statue within the "Greek Temple" is that of "Liberty in Distress". Cost of the monument was $97,000.

The huge block of Vermont marble on which the statue stands cost $3,200, making the total cost, including architect's fee, a bit more than $126,000! It is 124 feet in diameter with 16 Doric columns set around the outside with the names of World War battles cut into the frieze. At this writing, a movement is afoot to relocate the monument in a nearby park, because of the increase in traffic entering the city, but the cost of the project is holding it up.

Atlantic Foto Service. Published by Saltzburg's Merchandise Co., Atlantic City, N. J.

That same year, another important edifice was dedicated . . . Atlantic City Senior High School, just opposite that monument, on September 22. Student capacity was 2100 and the building cost $2,500,000. The school's pipe organ boasted six-thousand pipes and was said to be the fourth largest such instrument in the world! It has long since been dismantled and is now owned by a private collector in the west, who is restoring it.

In 1923, Atlantic City was enjoying good times as thousands of visitors converged on the resort for conventions and just plain sightseeing, via train, bus and car. People purchased toilet articles from their "Larkin man" who carried such items as talcum powder for only 25¢ for a 3-ounce sifter can; a double rouge compact for $1.20; face powder: 40¢ for a two-ounce box and lipstick for 25¢!

Atlantic City's first radio station, WHAR went on the air, with studios in the Seaside Hotel. It operated for a period of only two or three years. Two of its chief engineers were William Paulus and Earle Godfrey.

Shopping centers were unheard of and almost every neighborhood in town had grocery stores and butcher shops within easy reach. The American Stores Company had five outlets here: one at 300 Atlantic Avenue; another at 1931 Atlantic; one at 1007 Pacific Avenue; a store at 3010 Atlantic and one at 6500 Ventnor Avenue. And they offered such values as Asco coffee at 29¢ a pound, Victor bread, 5¢ a loaf. And if you wanted it wrapped, it cost you 9¢! If you were in the market for a new car, you probably included in your rounds of the dealerships, a visit to your friendly Hudson-Essex showroom at Antrim Motors, 40 N. Albany Avenue.

Two of Atlantic City's leading pharmacies were Cotton and Ackley's, 1701 Atlantic Avenue, and Wright's, Virginia and Atlantic. The Municipal Produce Market was opened on Absecon Boulevard that August. Prior to this time, farmers had sold their fruits and vegetables at a makeshift market at Florida and Fairmount Avenues, for many years. The first Market Master was Horace Ireland.

An important milestone for motorists in our town occurred this year, when the first traffic signal lights were installed at the intersection of Tennessee and Atlantic Avenues, and at Tennessee and Pacific Avenues. They were simply semaphores operated manually by the traffic officer on duty. Early photographs showing the lights in operation bear the caption "a new type of traffic signal operated from a tower erected at the corner of the intersection and manned by one of Atlantic City's finest."

All around the town, the newest songs were heard in cabarets, music stores and piers, including "Who's Sorry Now", "I Cried For You", "Yes! We Have No Bananas", "That Old Gang Of Mine", and "It Ain't Gonna Rain No Mo'."

A busy intersection in 1923: Tennessee and Pacific Avenues, showing the new traffic signals just above the head of the officer on the street. Note the other policeman in the tower, which would soon be phased out in favor of the newer device.

1924

Students at Atlantic City High School had good reason to be elated when their swimming team, dubbed "The Wonder Mermen", traveled to Northwestern University and won the National High School Swimming Championship. Al Turner, Dick Bew, Gus Bring and Gordy Yates set a relay record that, so far as we can learn, stands today! In golf, Leo Frazer, President of the Atlantic City Country Club and former P.G.A. President, was captain of the first golf team at A.C.H.S. in 1924.

On November 17, a three-alarm fire badly damaged four hotels; The Bothwell, The Wiltshire, The Senator and The Seaside. The same blaze gutted the entrance to Steel Pier. It was the first such fire in 17 years. Repairs to the pier involved enclosing the arcade so that it might be used for exhibits already booked, such as the Atlantic City Motor Trades Association Show.

Ruth Malcolmson, a lovely 16-year old brunette, who entered the Miss America Pageant as "Miss Philadelphia", was the reigning Miss America and received a snazzy new Dagmar automobile to use in making personal appearances.

1924 saw the Republican party in Atlantic City split into two factions, headed by Edward L. Bader and Harry Bacharach, respectively. Only ten candidates were voted upon that year, and the Bader Republicans placed one Democrat on their ticket. The law had been changed so that voters now balloted directly for a Mayor. The winning ticket was elected on May 13, and took their seats the following Tuesday: Bader as Mayor, Anthony M. Ruffu, William S. Cuthbert, Harry Headley and Louis Kuehnle.

The All-Wars Memorial Building, States and Pacific Avenues, built by the city as a headquarters for all veteran's activities, opened in April.

The legendary Norman Brokenshire,
Chief Announcer, WPG, circa 1926.

Songs published that year include "I Wonder What's Become Of Sally?", "I'll See You In My Dreams", "It Had To Be You", "Tea For Two" and "Your Lips Tell Me No, No But There's Yes, Yes In Your Eyes".

During the Memorial Day weekend, also known as "Decoration Day" back then, tourists visiting the World's Playground had their choice of a number of hotels for as little as $12 for Thursday through Sunday! And that included your meals! Among those hotels were the Bouvier, the Kenderton and the Osborne. One could stay at the Netherland from Thursday through Monday for $15! And at the Albemarle, now the site of a parking lot at Virginia and Pacific Avenues, your three-day stay cost only $5, but that was for your room only! Other Atlantic City hostelries advertising on the amusements and resorts pages of the old Philadelphia Public Ledger for May 29, 1924, included the Traymore, Edison, Thouron Manor, Healy's, Kentucky, Creston, Clarendon, Walter, New England, Watkins, New Davenport, Shoreham, Green's, Castro's, Grand Atlantic, Bingham, Boscobel and Lexington.

1925

People flocked to Atlantic City in the summer of '25 to see the beautiful new additions to two of Atlantic City's fine hotels. And the trip offered an opportunity for them to use the newly-opened Absecon Boulevard. Work on the roadway had begun in 1916 at the Absecon end but had to be interrupted during the World War in 1917-1918. It had been completed as a gravel surface highway and opened in December of 1919, but with more and more traffic coming into town, authorities realized it should be paved and so it was, with a bituminous compound.

Upon their arrival here, visitors hastened to inspect the new 245-room, two-million dollar addition to the Dennis Hotel, then owned by Walter J. Buzby. And the New Iroquois Hotel re-opened in July with a $300,000 addition!

A new development, "Atlantic City Terrace", located between Margate and Longport was advertising lots as low as $805 and sold 1,024 of them in a 4-week period! There was much building going on, and the business community reported an increase of 30% over the previous year!

An ordinance introduced by Mayor Bader called for the removal of screens, opaque glass and other such shields which would obstruct the view of the public into saloons, cafes, cigar stores and pool rooms. Proprietors of such establishments rebelled but it was the law and they complied rather than face fines.

We had more than our share of entertainment in that wonderful year! The nationally-famous Coon-Sanders Orchestra, billed as "The Original Kansas City Nighthawks", was appearing on the Million Dollar Pier, along with Charlie Fry leading the house band. At the Beaux Arts, on the Boardwalk at Virginia Avenue, the musical revue "Wild Waves of 1925" was a big draw.

In October, Billie Burke and Ernest Truex appeared on stage at Nixon's Apollo Theatre in "Annie Dear", followed the next week by "The Goose Hangs High". The Apollo was a pre-Broadway house and many were the dazzling shows that graced its stage prior to moving on to New York!

On July 4th, Sigmund Romberg's spectacular operetta, "The Student Prince" opened on Garden Pier.

P.C.D. Co. Made in U.S.A. - C. T. American Art.

At the movies, still silent, people went to see "Smoldering Fires" with Laura La Plante at the Bijou, "My Son", starring the great Nazimova at the Virginia, and Bebe Daniels in "The Crowded Hour", at the Colonial. And a beautiful new movie house opened on the boards at Kentucky Avenue! It was the Stanley which presented its initial offering on July 3, entitled "Are Parents People?" starring Adolphe Menjou and Florence Vidor.

This may surprise you, but parking was becoming a problem even then! To resolve the dilemma, resort officials were considering developing a 50-acre tract on the northside of town for free parking for our visitors! Yes, free! Whether the scheme ever got off the ground, we don't know. But a story in the Daily Press and Atlantic City Gazette listed all the details.

The new Chrysler, now in its second year, was selling for $895 at Bateman and Mixner, 816 Arctic Avenue. Our town hosted an international track meet, sponsored by the Kiwanis Club, that summer. It featured Oxford and Cambridge, England, versus Princeton and Cornell, at the airport on Albany Avenue, and the Englishmen won!

Nowadays, when most radio stations operate 24-hours a day, it's interesting to note that our city's two stations in 1925, WHAR and WPG, the new Municipal Station, had what were called "silent" days, with no broadcasting at all!

A few of 1925's song hits which remain popular today include, "Five Foot Two, Eyes Of Blue", "Dinah", "Moonlight And Roses", "Sleepy Time Gal", and "Sweet Georgia Brown".

No Publisher listed.

1926

Just as they are today, conventions in 1926 were very important to the economy of Atlantic City. We welcomed more than 400 gatherings that year, including 12,000 shriners, 1,200 delegates to the General Federation of Women's Clubs and almost ten-thousand delegates to the National Electric Light Association. Several cabinet members from The White House addressed gatherings here. And Thomas Alva Edison attended his first convention, in many a year, when he appeared at the Electric Light conclave here. From many standpoints, 1926 was a most progressive year in Atlantic City! Its popularity as the playground of the world was attested by the influx of visitors to the tune of 12-million!

The resulting effect on business was reflected in record bank clearings for the year of more than one-million dollars, per day! On Labor Day weekend, the crowd in town was estimated at well over 400,000! At Easter, 250,000 strollers paraded the boardwalk. The announcement that several large beachfront and side-avenue hotels would be built for the following season was welcomed with joy in all sectors of the city. The President Hotel had already opened and the Shelburne and Chelsea Hotels had built substantial additions to their existing premises, as had the Knickerbocker and others. The St. Charles was completing a new wing in 1926, and the Seaside had begun new construction. That same year, the new Colton Manor and Lafayette were begun.

The Miss America Pageant outdid all of its predecessors in 1926 when it brought together beauties from 73 cities in the U.S.A., Canada and Australia, culminating in the selection and crowning of lovely Norma Smallwood of Tulsa, Oklahoma. Some 30,000 persons viewed the afternoon parade. That event did not become the illuminated nighttime extravaganza it is today, until the 50's.

The Steel Pier's "Summer of 1926" program lists John Philip Sousa and his famous band during the month of July, along with Conway and his Band at concerts mornings at 11:15, afternoons at 3:30 and evenings at 8:30, in the Music Hall. Marjorie Moody, soprano and John Dolan, cornetist were featured with Sousa. The Casa Valencia, the summer restaurant at the Ritz Carlton Hotel, starred Gus Edwards and his "Ritz Carlton Nights" revue. Martin's, at New York Avenue and the 'Walk, was presenting Evelyn Nesbit, "The Girl In The Red Velvet Swing", plus Thelma Carlton, star of "Artists and Models". And La Victoire, on the Boardwalk opposite Steel Pier, was advertised as "Atlantic City's Finest Restaurant", where the blue plate seafood special was yours for only $1.50!

Our boardwalk has long been known for unique attractions and one of the most unusual was the Infant Incubator Exhibit at 2101 Boardwalk opposite Million Dollar Pier! There one could view tiny human babies in their incubators watched over by nurses, at all times.

When one wished to ride rather than walk, there was a fleet of "luxurious Pierce-Arrow buses" operated by the Absecon Bus Company from North Carolina Avenue and the beach, ready to carry you on a delightful sightseeing tour of the Island! Radio station WPG, the city-owned outlet, put on a 9-hour program in celebration of its first anniversary, on January 4, 1926, offering 2,000 prizes to the first two-thousand persons responding. Telegrams and letters arrived at the studios from 25,000 listeners throughout the nation and the world! On the night of August 2, the famous movie idol, Rudolph Valentino gave his last public talk before his untimely death, in the WPG Marine Studio on Steel Pier.

Movie-goers thrilled to the antics of Harold Lloyd and his college chums in "The Freshman", and Charlie Chaplin, the little man with the cane and the funny walk, in "The Gold Rush". In sports, Georges Carpentier trained for his boxing bout with Tommy Loughran, while Jack Dempsey was in training here for his fight with Gene Tunney.

Some of the songs being hummed and sung were "The Blue Room", "Gimme a Little Kiss, Will Ya, Huh", "Baby Face", "It All Depends On You", and "Breezin' Along With The Breeze."

And many localities traveled to Philadelphia to enjoy the Sesqui-Centennial celebration that year.

1927

The big story of 1927 was the solo flight across the Atlantic Ocean by a tall, shy young man named Charles A. Lindbergh, in his little Ryan monoplane "The Spirit of St. Louis", in May. When word was flashed to the world that the "Lone Eagle" had made it to Paris, Atlantic City celebrated for days! He later visited here.

At Nixon's Apollo Theatre, Grace George opened in "The Legend of Lenora" the week of March 21; "My Maryland" played there the week of January 10; Blanche Ring starred on the Apollo stage in "Cradle Snatchers" for a week starting January 24; and "The Circus Princess", a lavish production with a cast of hundreds, played that famous house the week of April 4, 1927.

Just before Christmas, the Masonic Temple, Hartford and Ventnor Avenues, was dedicated. It has a seating capacity of 1200. The cornerstone, brought from the legendary quarries of King Solomon's mines, was laid with a trowel used by George Washington for the cornerstone at the nation's capitol.

Published by General Merchandise Co., Atlantic City, N. J.

Resort theatres showing "photoplays" included the Woods, Boardwalk at Ocean Avenue; The Central, 2416 Atlantic Avenue; The Bijou, Boardwalk at South Carolina; The City Square, 1318 Atlantic Avenue; The Criterion, Boardwalk near Virginia; The Park, Ohio and Atlantic; The Royal, Atlantic Avenue near Kentucky and the Globe, on the Boardwalk at Delaware Avenue. The Globe later became a top burlesque house.

Local music shoppes and 5 & 10 cent stores featured sheet music and records of such songs as "Blue Skies", "Side By Side", "Ramona", "Make Believe", "Me And My Shadow" and "The Varsity Drag".

Also in 1927, The Boardwalk National Bank Arcade, on the 'Walk between Tennessee and Ocean Avenues, opened. The first large structure on this site was Kipple and McCann's Baths and Roof Garden, at Ocean Avenue with Ye Olde Mill, an amusement center, at Tennessee Avenue.

Miss Atlantic City, lovely Eleanor Hoffman, was married in December, in New York City, to John F. Strauss, Jr. Congressman Isaac Bacharach, of Atlantic City, was the guest of President Calvin Coolidge at breakfast in the White House, in Washington.

The National Kennel Club held whippet races on a track laid out at Tennessee Avenue and Absecon Boulevard. 144 dogs participated in the inaugural event on July 16. However, the attraction folded the following month, when the promoters claimed they'd lost $35,000 in the venture. Dody Cicero, star athlete at Holy Spirit High School, left town to sign a contract with the Boston Red Sox baseball team.

To give you an idea of prices that year, Schwartz Brothers, 1619

Atlantic Avenue was advertising ladies' silk hosiery at $1.50 a pair; handbags for $2.95 and men's pajamas for $1.98. Kensington Carpet Company, then located at Kentucky and Atlantic Avenues, was the "authorized dealers for Atwater Kent and Zenith radios". F. A. North, 2632 Atlantic Avenue, was agent for the Lester Player Piano. Remember how we inserted a paper roll with little holes in it, and out came beautiful music . . . when we pumped the pedals?

Local banking institutions mailed out $1,185,000 in Christmas Club checks that December and City Commissioner William S. Cuthbert appointed 17 additional policemen to form an "Owl Watch" in the city; starting salary was $2,200.

1928

The excursion steamer "Atlantic Beach Park" was wrecked on the beach near Morris Avenue during a 65-mile-an-hour gale, in April. The vessel was under tow from New York. Three persons, including the Captain, were lost when their lifeboat was swamped by mountainous waves. Four others were rescued by Captains Harry Yates and Richard Hughes of the Beach Patrol, who brought a lifeboat a distance of more than a mile to the scene!

And 1928 saw another boardwalk fire, just after the New Year began. Flames enveloped Richards' and Cuthberts' Baths and The Atlantic Foto Gallery at South Carolina Avenue, on January 29th. Public Safety Director William S. Cuthbert, who set a record for attendance at practically every big fire in the city for more than half a century, was out of town at the time, but was summoned here by phone. On another occasion, the director's home was threatened by fire while he was out to dinner and he knew nothing about it til it was over. But he made most of the others!

The Y.W.C.A. Building at North Carolina and Pacific Avenues, which was razed in 1978, was erected in 1928 at a cost of half-a-million pre-depression dollars! It was designed in Gothic style by Vaughan Mathis, Architect, with Philip G. Hannum, General Contractor. The structure was five stories high, and contained an auditorium, gymnasium, cafeteria, sleeping quarters, offices, library, meeting rooms and lounges. In the early 70's, the building was taken over by the Reverend Carl McIntyre and used as his Atlantic City headquarters.

There were many clubs and civic associations then about which we hear nothing today. Among those active were the Caledonian Club, Cosmopolitan Club, Hygeia Swimming Club, Lu Lu Yacht Club, Turner Maennerchor, The Heralds of Liberty, The Old Colony Club, and Ye Rod and Reel Club. And, of course, Atlantic City had its organization made up of Civil War veterans of the Grand Army of the Republic, the famed G.A.R.

This was the year the Morris Guards, a local fraternal organization, put on its own production of Rudolph Friml's "The Firefly" at the Globe Theatre on the Boardwalk in February. Many localites appeared behind the footlights in a lavish show staged by Frank W. Shea! Included in the cast were George Swinton, Stephen A. Damico, Harry Smith,

Walter W. Clark Jr., John Boucher, Ward Eldredge, Edison Hedges, Joseph Walker, Gladys Mathis, Christine Chapman and Alice Burch. The orchestra was under the baton of Joseph Abrams.

Song hits of 1928 include "Carolina Moon", "Button Up Your Overcoat", "I'll Get By", "Makin' Whoopee" and the novelty tune "I Faw Down And Go Boom". During the week of March 5, Nixon's Apollo presented "The Desert Song" as America and Atlantic City laughed and played, blissfully unaware of the sadness the following year would bring.

1929

The very first dial telephone call in Atlantic City was made on March 3, 1929, when Mayor Anthony Ruffu, sitting in the editorial offices of the Press-Union Newspapers at midnight, received a call from Walter J. Buzby, marking the switchover from manual to dial phones. That same year saw the first ship-to-shore telephone call from Atlantic City to a vessel on the high seas. William Rankin, President of a New York advertising agency, made the call from the Chalfonte Hotel that December, to yachtsman Sir Thomas Lipton on board the liner "Leviathan", 200 miles at sea!

In September, a beginning was made on construction of a cutoff highway from Shore Road at Tuckerton across to Brigantine, and thence into Atlantic City, which was expected to shorten the trip from New York City by some 12 miles. By the time a gravel road had been built to the edge of Great Bay, financing problems arose and nothing further was done, but it was a good idea.

Street cars, including the famous "summer cars", which were open on the sides, continued as a popular and economical mode of transportation here. Fares on local trolleys to Margate and Longport were reduced to seven cents from 14 cents in April. That's correct: reduced!

Published by H. S. Sampliner, Atlantic City, N. J. Natural Color Post Card Made in U.S.A. by E. C. Kropp Co., Milwaukee, Wis.

Hundreds of show business openings have taken place in Atlantic City, and 1929 had more than its share! The new Auditorium saw the opening of the production "Here and There", while Fred Allen and Clifton Webb appeared in "The Little Show". Other luminaries making their Atlantic City debuts that memorable year were Joe Cook, Lionel Atwill, and Spencer Tracy, on Garden Pier. One of the year's top shows, "Rio Rita" played the summer of '29 on that pier and the one and only Mae West starred, in person, in "Diamond Lil", at the old Globe Theatre on the Boardwalk at Maryland Avenue.

30,000 persons witnessed the dedication of our new Convention Hall, in June. Vice-President of the United States, Charles Curtis, was one of the principal speakers and Mayor Ruffu was the Master of Ceremonies. "A Temple Of World Peace" . . . "The Geneva Of The Americas" . . . that was the prophecy of national and world statesmen at the opening of the new $15,000,000 structure, at Georgia Avenue and the Boardwalk.

Seats in the world's largest auditorium were available mainly in the balcony, due to the National Electric Light Association exhibits being set up. The big show got underway at 10 P.M. and the hall's General Manager, Lincoln G. Dickey was a very proud man as he viewed the culmination of years of planning and construction. Two U.S. Navy units played important roles in the dedication. The battleship U.S.S. Wyoming, anchored offshore, fired a salute from her 16-inch guns to honor the Vice-President, while the dirigible, U.S.S. Los Angeles, moved silently overhead, then sounded a siren setting off an "electric ear" on the ground, which automatically threw a switch. This turned on the exterior lighting of the great hall, creating an "Aurora Borealis" effect!

Genuine Curteich-Chicago "C. T. Art-Colortone" Post Card (Reg. U.S. Pat. Off.) Jersey Supply Company, Atlantic City, N. J.

When folks gathered around the old piano in the parlor, someone in the group was almost certain to suggest one or more of these current hits: "You're The Cream In My Coffee", "That's My Weakness Now", "I'm A Dreamer, Aren't We All", "Painting The Clouds With Sunshine", and "Stardust".

In local sports, Atlantic City High School's famed basketball team went to the state championship finals for the first time in its history. Although A.C.H.S. lost to Passaic High in the Trenton Armory, George McMillan and Leo Keating were named to the first team, all-state!

Ray Keech, who once drove a gasoline truck in Atlantic City, won the famous Indianapolis Speedway Memorial Day Classic, in May, driving a Miller race car, and was clocked at a speed of 97.585 miles an hour!

As part of the celebration of the Golden Jubilee of the incandescent lamp, the fountain of light in Brighton Park on the Boardwalk was erected by General Electric at a cost of $25,000. It was given to the city on the 50th anniversary of the invention of the lamp by New Jersey's Thomas A. Edison. The fountain is 18 feet wide and 10 feet high with jets spurting water to heights of 15, 20 and 30 feet. 30 lamps at its base have color screens to provide more than 70 different color combinations!

The inaugural program of our beautiful new Warner Theatre, for its premier performance June 19, 1929, featured the playing of our national anthem by the Warner Theatre Orchestra, conducted by Charles Previn. Following the dedication, short addresses were delivered by Mayor Ruffu, Warner Brothers Pictures' President, H. M. Warner and New Jersey Governor Morgan F. Larson. Then the audience settled back in those big, comfortable seats to enjoy the screen presentation, "On With The Show", the first 100% natural color talking, singing, dancing picture, a Vitaphone production in Technicolor, the latest advancement in motion picture technology! Featured in the film were Betty Compson, Louise Fazenda, Sally O'Neill, Joe E. Brown and Ethel Waters.

Published by H. S. Sampliner, Atlantic City, N. J. Natural Post Card Made in U.S.A. by E. C. Kroop Co., Milwaukee, Wis. (Edy).

I remember the Warner so well. We could look up at the vaulted ceiling and see what appeared to be tiny stars twinkling in a sky of deep blue, creating the illusion of being outdoors! And the acoustics at the Warner left nothing to be desired! It was truly a world apart, an escape from reality, if you please, and the opening of that dazzling showplace was a major topic of conversation for weeks! Admissions ranged from 40¢ daily to 85¢ for weekends!

Its name was later changed to the Warren, simply by rearranging the letters. And the ornate structure ended its days as a bowling emporium, Boardwalk Lanes! Part of its facade remains today.

And a national event, which was naturally reflected in resort business, took place that October when the economy of the nation reached the point where the bottom dropped out and the market crash occurred. Many a localite was literally wiped out financially, and the year ended on the down-side.

1930

"Shipwreck Kelly". What memories that name conjures up! Do you recall when he sat atop a flagpole on Steel Pier for 49 days and one hour back in 1930? Billed as "The Luckiest Fool Alive", Alvin "Shipwreck" Kelly took five minute catnaps on the hour to retain his strength. His fee: $100 per day! When he ended his stint on the swaying pole, it was only because he missed his wife! After 1,177 hours, and three thunderstorms and a hail storm, Kelly descended as 20,000 well-wishers cheered from the beach and boardwalk.

To make his sitting a bit more comfortable, Kelly sat on a padded eight-inch automobile brake drum! Whatever happened to "Shipwreck" Kelly? He was found dead on a New York City street in October of 1952. Yellowed newspaper clippings on the body identified him as the famed daredevil who had once thrilled millions all over America, including spellbound crowds in Atlantic City, in the 30's.

"Monopoly", one of the great parlor games of all time, vying with Scrabble and Parchesi for popularity, has made Atlantic City real estate familiar to millions of game fans the world over! It was the invention of Charles Darrow and his wife, who resided in Philadelphia, when he reportedly got the idea for the game, in 1930.

Darrow thought it would be a good way to help people forget their cares and woes during the depression which then gripped America. The inventor's reason for using Atlantic City as the game's locale. The city was, at that time, world-renowned for its pleasures and opulence. Parker Brothers marketed the game and the rest is history!

To date, "Monopoly" has sold close to 100,000,000 sets! For Darrow, it was a one-time shot. He never devised another successful game. An effort to change the names of some of Atlantic City's streets, which appear on the game board, failed a number of years ago when Monopoly fans strongly objected!

The Second National Bank, Atlantic and New York Avenues, was advertising a capital of $300,000, resources of more than $6,000,000 and

4% interest on savings, in 1930.

Bershad's Baths, 519-25 Boardwalk was advertised as "The Carlsbad of America", featuring hot salt water baths, Swedish massage and sun ray treatments. A local taxi company advertised rates for one or two persons at just 50¢ . . . each additional: 25¢! And there was a least one telephone answering service in the resort 50 years ago!

The American Automobile Association, as a national body, was voicing opposition to toll roads, and the Atlantic City Chapter went on record as favoring an express highway between Camden and Atlantic City. Reduced fares to Philadelphia via Quaker City Bus Lines were one dollar, one way . . . $1.50 round trip!

Burt Radio, on Atlantic Avenue, offered sales and service on the latest receivers by Majestic, Atwater Kent, RCA Radiola, and Sparton. And the bridge over the Inside Thorofare at Dorset Avenue, in Ventnor, connecting that city with Ventnor Heights, opened to traffic on May 29, just in time for the Memorial Day rush!

Earl Johnson of Williamstown, founded the Lincoln Transit Company in 1930, at the International Garage, 2211 Atlantic Avenue, operating buses between here and New York City.

At the Liberty Theatre, Jack Holt was featured in "Flight", while at the Royal, one could see "Hit The Deck", with Winnie Lightner and Jack Oakie.

Some of the tunes which helped folks shake those depression blues included, "Happy Days Are Here Again", "Bye Bye Blues", "For You", "Three Litle Words" and "Fine And Dandy".

1931

Was it a bird? Was it a plane? How about a rocket glider? Yes, that's what cheering spectators saw on June 4, 1931, here in Atlantic City, when William G. Swann, a 29-year old local stunt flyer piloted what was reputed to be the first rocket glider in the history of aviation, from the Steel Pier! Only a single rocket was used and it carried the craft, with Swann at the controls, a distance of 1,000 feet at an altitude of 100 feet. The glider had been built as a pier attraction, just one of many when that showplace was under the aegis of Frank P. Gravatt. Does anyone know whatever became of it?

Automobile prices weren't always what they are nowadays. True, many refinements have been added over the years, but just the same, back in 1931, the price of a new Chevrolet ran from $510 to $635 for a deluxe model! And the now-famous and sought-after Model A Ford, the darling of many old car collectors, was selling new for $435 to $600, fully equipped! A new Plymouth cost between $565 and $625, and if you wanted real class, a 1930 Buick was yours for a tad over $1,000.

If you owned a car at that time, you might recall the Times Square Auto Supply, 1729 Atlantic Avenue. They were advertising car batteries for $3.29, auto robes to keep you warm for 79¢, fender guides (remember them, dad?) for 9¢ and their famous "Red Cat" heater for all cars, priced at an amazing $2.09!

1931's woman could get machine-type permanent waves in Atlantic City beauty shops for $3.50, and if she took along a lady friend, the waves were priced at two for $6! The old M. E. Blatt Department Store, South Carolina and Atlantic Avenues, was selling boy's corduroy knickers for $1.79. Remember the rubbing sound they made as we walked? Lumber jackets were $1.98 and men's suits and topcoats, both for $39.50! Ladies' polo coats with large collar and lapels were only $16.50 and rayon berets cost just 19¢.

This was the year our Police Department was first connected with the New Jersey State Police via teletype so that multi-state alarms could be sent out on stolen cars and other criminal matters.

And you won't believe these prices on groceries in '31! But, so help me, they appear in a copy of the old Atlantic City Evening Union from August of that year. Wagenheim's Meat Market on North Kentucky Avenue was selling prime sirloin steak for 28¢ a pound, fresh pork chops at 24¢ a pound, sugar-cured hams for 17¢ a pound, and creamery butter for 35¢ a pound! Gordon's Meats, 1206 Atlantic Avenue, advertised spring lamb at a nickel a pound, and corned beef for 25¢ a pound!

Dancer Bill "Bojangles" Robinson played the Globe Theatre that year in a revue called "Hot From Harlem", which featured Eubie Blake and his Radio Orchestra. Admission was 50¢! George White's "Scandals" starring Rudy Vallee and Ray Bolger, played Garden Pier. The Atlantic City Casino on Absecon Boulevard offered a 7-course dinner, plus a big show, for one dollar! Rum runners were boasting they had no trouble getting the stuff into Atlantic City, except for the Coast Guard, now and then. The law clamped down on six bus companies whose drivers had been arrested for traveling 45 to 60 MPH when the speed limit on the pike was 40!

If you wanted to visit New York to see a show, the bus would take you there and bring you back to Atlantic City for only $3.75. Yes, that's round trip! Should you desire to travel to Norfolk, Virginia, for the Yorktown Sesqui-Centennial, the cost was $7 round trip, via train between here and there!

Industrial leaders were seeking ways and means to cure the depression, while local banks were jubilant over the $250,000 increase in deposits during the Columbus Day holiday, over the same period the previous year! We had a population then of some 66,000!

As the Nation and Atlantic City struggled under great economic strain, singing helped make life a bit more bearable, and the songs were beautiful! They included "Heartaches", "Got A Date With An Angel", "I Surrender, Dear", "Goodnight Sweetheart" and "Love Letters In The Sand".

1932

Dance marathons were popular in 1932, and the Million Dollar Pier attracted large crowds who sat or stood and watched exhausted dancers holding each other up, but somehow managing to move around the floor in a valiant effort to win some cash. The nation was deep in the depression and money was hard to come by for most of us. From an old photo post card, we learn that six winning teams that season were Mary Fenton and Joie Ray, Mr. and Mrs. Fred Curio, who, by the way, were married during the marathon, Josephine Pingo and Billy Cavanaugh, Billy Reeves and Harry Reeves, Pearl Jouet and Jimmy Barrett, and Ruth Smith and Frank Lovecchio. Lovecchio went on to fame and fortune as a singer after changing his name to . . . Frankie Laine!

Those six teams had kept their feet moving for a total of 130 days, or 3,120 hours! During most of the decade, dance marathons and walkathons were the rage here, along the Jersey Shore, and Atlantic City was really caught up in the excitement!

The year produced some really great songs, such as "Brother, Can You Spare A Dime?", "Forty-Second Street", "Please", "Say It Isn't So" and "Night And Day".

Most everyone was a radio fan! Top shows included "The Panatela Program", which featured a couple of newcomers to the airwaves, George Burns and Gracie Allen! After hearing them on the air, Guy Lombardo signed them up to appear on his weekly show. Ben Bernie And All The Lads was sponsored by Pabst Blue Ribbon and his popular "Yowsah, Yowsah" became a household phrase.

Comedy shows were big, with "Fibber McGee and Molly", Weber and Fields, and Ed Wynn, "The Perfect Fool".

A three-bedroom and bath apartment, complete with janitor service and heat, was renting in Atlantic City for $35 a month! A six-room house in Bungalow Park rented for $37 monthly. And on South Little Rock Avenue, one could rent a store for only $25 a month! Souder Motors was our Hudson-Essex dealer at 40 N. Albany Avenue, and the new six-cylinder Chevrolet was on display at Cuskaden, 2600 Atlantic Avenue. S. L. Walden, 114 S. New York Avenue, was Atlantic City's Ford dealer, introducing that sensational new V-8, in 1932, after Henry dropped the Model A.

Meteorologist Samuel Deitch, now retired, took charge of the Atlantic City Weather Bureau, then located on Rhode Island Avenue. Fire destroyed the famed Steeplechase Pier on Valentine's Day, 1932, Professor A. F. Seward, billed as "The World's Foremost Astrologer", maintained studios at 1541 Boardwalk, where people could learn if the prosperity, which politicians were saying was "just around the corner", held any promise for them. Of 20 candidates in the sixth commission election that May, these men were seated on the 17th: Harry Bacharach, Joseph Paxson, William S. Cuthbert, Robert L. Warke and Louis Kuehnle.

1933

The city and the nation were just beginning to recover from the effects of the great depression, but it was a slow process! Thousands were unemployed, but somehow folks scraped up enough cash to escape the realities and hardships of life and play for awhile!

On Memorial Day weekend, the famous Paul Whiteman, "The King of Jazz", brought his orchestra to Steel Pier where it alternated in the

Marine Ballroom with Alex Bartha's band. Some of the current songs they probably featured were, "Let's Fall In Love", "Fit As A Fiddle And Ready For Love", "Just A Little Sweet Where Old Friends Meet", "Say It Isn't So" and "We're In The Money", which was just wishful thinking for most people, in 1933.

The reigning Miss America was a 16-year old blonde from Connecticut, Marion R. Bergeron. After this Pageant, there would be a period of two years before the event was renewed. Also in the beauty department, Ruth Leroy was the current Miss Atlantic City.

A local tax relief committee was suggesting the elimination of two ladder companies and three engine companies as a means of cutting taxes, but they didn't want the safety of the public jeopardized. You couldn't buy beer legally so people made their own, and sometimes it wasn't too bad! They called it "Home Brew" and the makings could be purchased at your food store, including the A&P. What you bought was malt syrup such as "Old Munich" at 45¢ a can, or "Buckeye", "Blue Ribbon" and "Budweiser" at 59¢ a can. Following directions, and each household seemed to have its own special recipe, it was mixed in a big earthenware crock, then bottled and allowed to "age". If the yeast content was too high, caps could be heard popping at all hours, down in the basement!

Meanwhile, in Trenton, Atlantic County Assemblyman Siracusa was planning to introduce a bill which would give municipal governing bodies in the state absolute control over retail beer sales and taxation.

Perhaps you recall being paid in scrip, a form of legal tender authorized for paying salaries, on February 9, 1933. Total amount paid out in Atlantic City was $9,483,048. When it was redeemed, $3,762 was unaccounted for and it's believed to be in existence today as a memento of those sad depression days of the 30's.

The old Atlantic City Lighthouse was decommissioned on July 11, after a 70-foot tall steel tower had been erected at the foot of New Hampshire Avenue at the Boardwalk, which was first lighted on June 9th.

Rudy Vallee and his Connecticut Yankees, with Rudy at the front of the band complete with megaphone, played Atlantic City in '33. His name had become a household word following such smash hits as "The Maine Stein Song", "I'm Just A Vagabond Lover", and "My Time Is Your Time", his haunting theme song.

And this was the year that saw the Pennsylvania Reading Seashore Lines created by the merger of the old West Jersey and Seashore Railroad with the Philadelphia and Atlantic City Line, in June.

Those who were working tried to help those who weren't, and even at prices unrealistic by today's standards, it wasn't easy to keep food on the table unless one worked out a budget. Coffee sold for 17¢ a pound, salad dressing: 29¢ a quart, peaches were six pounds for 29¢, Raisin Bran: two 10-ounce packages for 21¢, sugar corn: six ears for 13¢ and luncheon meats: 5¢ for a quarter-pound!

What went wrong?

1934

Our Police Department began using prowl cars in August. These special vehicles were equipped with two-way radios made by the department's wireless technician, Lawrence J. Smith. Smith was the first person in the nation to develop an efficient pocket-size radio for use by motorcycle police and foot patrolmen, making them well-equipped for handling emergencies. Today's sophisticated radio gear has come a long way since those early sets developed by Lawrence Smith right in the shops of the local Police Department.

Our new $250,000 railroad depot at the Union Terminal of the Pennsylvania-Reading Seashore Lines was dedicated that year, with notables from all parts of the state in attendance. It was big news and made the November 8th issue of the Christian Science Monitor from which comes this account: "The building is modified classic in design, finished in granite, Indiana limestone and brick. Besides the Reading Terminal, the new station replaces the old Pennsylvania Railroad building, eight blocks away on South Carolina Avenue near Atlantic. This building was razed and the mile of trackage leading to it was torn up, eliminating 12 grade crossings and opening streets which formerly were dead ends. Eight trains of 16 cars each can stand side-by-side taking on or discharging passengers 10-thousand at a time!" This was proved time and time again during the summer of 1934.

Atlantic City Station, Pennsylvania-Reading Seashore Lines, as it appeared July 6, 1935. Collection of John Deysher.

The summer schedule of the Shore Fast Line, dated June 24, 1934, boasts "Every 30 minutes on the hour and half hour from both terminals, high speed electric trains between Atlantic City Terminal at Virginia Avenue and the Boardwalk and the Ocean City Terminal at 8th Street and the Boardwalk there".

Fare was 75¢ for the daily excursion, one-day round trip.

Emblazoned on the front of that time table is the famous N.R.A. insignia with the Blue Eagle and the words "We Do Our Part". Remember? The Shore Fast Line also ran buses painted orange, as was its other rolling stock. A 20-trip family ticket for use of purchaser or any member of the household cost $7 and was good for three months on either bus or train.

The song which won the Academy Award that year was "Carioca" from "The Gay Divorcee". Other hits of '34 include "Blue Moon", "I Get A Kick Out Of You", "With My Eyes Wide Open I'm Dreaming", "Santa Claus Is Coming To Town", and "The Very Thought Of You", composed by Atlantic County's Sidney Ascher.

We hear lots of discussion on how cold certain winters in Atlantic City have been, and many of them have gone into the record books, but the winter of 1934 wasn't exactly balmy! On February 9th, the mercury plummeted to minus nine degrees at 8 A.M., that's nine below zero! According to the Evening Union for the following day, representative readings for many area communities indicated the deep-freeze was far-reaching! Absecon reported 12 below and Somers Point, 19 below zero! And that cold snap lasted for 10 consecutive days!

1935

Atlantic City's Convention Hall has played host to thousands of conventions, some of which made little news, but in 1935 the big auditorium was the scene of a dramatic event which had nationwide repercussions and splashed the Atlantic City dateline on page one of newspapers from coast to coast!

John L. Lewis, the famed labor leader, raised a furor on the floor at the American Federation of Labor conclave in a heated argument, and the head of the United Mine Workers Union left the hall in anger, thereby causing a gigantic rift in the labor-union movement.

The fiery leader proceeded immediately to form the Congress of Industrial Organizations, the C.I.O., as a direct result of his battle here in Atlantic City in 1935!

Bacharach Boulevard was dedicated in October after the city had created the artery when the South Carolina Avenue Railroad Station was closed and the tracks ripped up.

You just may have been among the thousands who flocked to Steel Pier that summer to laugh and applaud a new comedian with a basket under his arm containing a live duck! He was Joe Penner who repeatedly asked, "Wanna Buy A Duck"? The zany phrase caught on and it was common to hear it almost everywhere.

On local movie screens, Dixie Lee and Burns and Allen appeared in "Love In Bloom", while William Powell, Myrna Loy and their pet dog "Asta", starred in "The Thin Man".

Dr. Allan Roy Dafoe, who became world famous almost overnight after delivering the Dionne quintuplets in Ontario, Canada, came to town to attend a medical convention and was recognized almost everywhere he went. Other V.I.P.'s visiting Atlantic City that year were stage, screen and radio star Al Jolson, author of dog stories, Albert Payson Terhune, and explorer and world-traveler Lincoln Ellsworth. John Edgar Hoover, famed Chief of the F.B.I. and Homer S. Cummings, Attorney General of the United States were staying at the Traymore. Both men were here to address the convention of the International Association of Chiefs of Police at the Ambassador.

That summer, the Atlantic City Regatta was held with 300 craft including the fastest boats along the Atlantic seaboard competing in 14 events. It took place at Beach Thorofare on June 28 and 29. It was directed by the Absecon Island Yacht Club and the South Jersey Speedboat Association. The outstanding event was a 25-mile marathon race for inboards for the S. Mortimer Auerbach Trophy. Fred Hahn, Rear Commodore of the local Yacht Club, served as General Chairman; Adrian Phillips was Vice-Chairman and Arno Apel was Secretary. So far as we can learn, the Regatta was short-lived, but gained much publicity just the same.

Another stellar attraction in the early season of 1935 was the Atlantic City Horse Show at Convention Hall! Arthur W. White was Ringmaster and officiated in the traditional grand style, including sounding the opening notes on the "Yard of Tin", that long, tapered horn used to signal the opening of equine events. The show actually had an "outside" type course for hunters, complete with hurdles for jumpers. A horse named "Cocobolo", a five-gaited saddle gelding, garnered many ribbons for its owner. Another feature of the big show was a six-horse hitch class, in which tons of horseflesh thundered around the ring inside Convention Hall!

On the Million Dollar Pier that fall, the Eastern League Basketball Contest between Atlantic City and Chester, Pennsylvania, with another game following, plus dancing afterwards, all for the single admission price of a quarter, must have really packed 'em in!

"Lullaby of Broadway" from "The Gold Diggers" won the Academy Award and some of the other songs that kept people cheerful as the Depression continued, were: "Beautiful Lady In Blue", "Begin The Beguine", "Cheek To Cheek", "I Can't Can't Get Started", and "On The Good Ship Lollipop", introduced by little Shirley Temple.

1936

It was the era of the big bands and each summer during the 30's, people flocked to the piers and hotels to actually see the orchestras they had heard so often on network broadcasts from New York, Chicago, Los Angeles and Atlantic City! Million Dollar Pier and Steel Pier featured just about all the big names including Benny Goodman, Jean Goldkette, Paul Whiteman, Rudy Vallee, Clyde McCoy, Hal Kemp, Ted Fio Rito, Abe Lyman and more!

In addition to the "name" bands that played Atlantic City, there were others which entertained year round. A WPG worksheet for the summer of '36 shows these "remote" pickups: Alex Bartha's Steel Pier Orchestra, Joe Briglia, Eddy Bradd, Don Hunt, Sid Berg, "Doc" Dougherty, Bert Estlow, Roger Kay, Joe Stern, Al Lewis, Eddy Morgan's Million

Dollar Pier Orchestra, William Madden, Charles Jones, Peter Russo, Al Geidt and Charles Hamer.

Then there were Harry Dobbs, Leonard Lewis, Al Miller, Frank Ritts, Oscar Petters' Admirals, Sid Rosen, Bob Brown, Joseph Gluck, Nick Kratka, John Peck, Benny Morris and Leo Sachs. These bands varied in size and played the local clubs, cabarets and hotel dining rooms.

Steel Pier, then under the aegis of the great entrepreneur Frank P. Gravatt, featured the top names of "stage, screen and radio" as the billing went in those days. On Labor Day weekend, 1936, there were four . . . count 'em . . . four bands playing in the Marine Ballroom: Mal Hallett, Ozzie Nelson, Frank Daily and his "Stop and Go Orchestra", and Atlantic City's own Alex Bartha, who fronted the house band at the pier until the early 50's.

There was continuous music from noon Sunday til 4 A.M. on Monday, Labor Day, and the ballroom was packed right up til that wee small hour, with the day's paid admissions tallying 74,800!

The General Motors Exhibit was a major Atlantic City attraction for years. But did you know that the Ford Motor Company also had an exhibit on Steel Pier in 1936? It was in the area later occupied by "Ocean Wonderworld" and fronted on the boardwalk. Foremost among its displays was "The Car In The Clouds", an arresting optical illusion featuring a lovely living model! There she was, seated behind the wheel of a beautiful blue 1936 Ford V-8 Roadster, appearing for all the world, to be riding a soft, fluffy cloud! The Jewel Room was another presentation of unusual beauty at the Ford Exhibit.

150 boys completed in a contest tied in with the legendary fisherman, Huckleberry Finn. It was the Traymore Hotel Mark Twain Memorial Pageant, part of a nationwide search for the best Mark Twain look-alike! Bill Ryerson was the winner here, Jack Higgins was runner-up and little Tommy Burns was the popular contestant with the crowds.

The event was held on the beach in front of the Traymore, our famous and lamented "Castle By The Sea", razed in 1972.

Construction work on the Atlantic City Post Office, at Illinois and Pacific Avenues, began in 1936 on the site of the first 100-foot tall hotel in the resort, built in 1890. It was the Garden Hotel, later known as Craig Hall. The Post Office cornerstone was laid on April 4, and the building opened to the public in February, 1937. Thomas Stewart was Postmaster.

The Atlantic City Tuna Club was founded that year. Its clubhouse at 741 N. Massachusetts Avenue burned in December of 1946, and its new facilities were opened in 1948.

Our seventh commission election was held on May 12, with 12 candidates vying for seats. The five winners were sworn in the following week: Charles D. White, Frank B. Off, William S. Cuthbert, William F. Casey and Joseph A. Paxson.

Starting in the fall of '36, football games were played indoors at Convention Hall. And our town played host to Rotary International's 27th Annual Convention with more than 14,000 in attendance. William S. Wilson was President of our Rotary Club.

Many great songs came out that year: "Moonlight and Shadows", "A Fine Romance", "The Glory of Love", "Stompin' At The Savoy" and "The Touch Of Your Lips", with lyrics by our own Sidney Ascher!

1937

A fire broke out on July 16 which has gone down in the annals of the local Fire Department as one of the worst holocausts on record! The story takes up a complete chapter in Franklin Kemp's fine book "Firefighting By The Seashore" under the title of "The Day It Rained Fire".

The location was Drexel and Virginia Avenues where the Pure Oil Company had a combination storage facility and service station. One hour after the box alarm was turned in at 1:15 P.M., the top of the largest tank gave way under pressure, letting loose a cloud of fire which shot upward more than a thousand feet! It then began to descend, taking oxygen away from the hundreds of spectators and firefighters at the scene.

Many people collapsed as the fire cloud settled, bringing with it heat which broke windows for a radius of a mile and scorched lawns and shrubbery! Total loss was placed at between $50,000 and $100,000!

On a happier note, a page one story in the Evening Union of August 16 tells of a "Million Dollar Crowd" over the weekend! "Hotels and rooming houses", reads the report, "were filled, and those unable to find lodging slept in their cars." Restaurants were doing capacity business, and our merchants were all smiles!

"The mass exodus by car and train", continues the article, "began at about 7 P.M. and continued long past midnight. All parking spaces on side streets, as well as most lots, were filled overnight on Saturday, and the line of cars on Sunday stretched from the Boardwalk to Mediterranean Avenue. Even Maine Avenue was jammed."

A group of national manufacturers commissioned William F. B. Koelle, a prominent Philadelphia architect, to design and construct "The Home of the Century" on Steel Pier for the summer of 1937. The building, which was visited by hundreds of thousands, was a two-story dwelling with just about every innovation available at the time, plus some which still were in the experimental stage!

It featured a tower staircase and balcony in the living room and its stained glass windows depicted knights and their ladies. And wait til you hear the price! According to a story in "Steel Pier Parade", a local publication of the period, "The Home of the Century" could be built for $7500! In 1939, the building was reproduced for the World's Fair in New York.

Memorial Day weekend saw three orchestras on Steel Pier: those of Benny Goodman, Guy Lombardo and the perennial Alex Bartha. In the Casino Theatre, audiences thrilled to "A Star Is Born" with Janet Gaynor and Frederic March on screen. On stage in the Music Hall was dancer Sally Rand of fan and bubble fame. And in the foyer at the pier's entrance, the "Aloha" spirit reigned as the Imperial Hawaiians dispensed beautiful music.

In sports, Garden Pier featured wrestling with the Dusek Brothers, Ernie and Joe; "Reb" Russell and Jack Donovan on the card. Admission was 55¢. The final meeting of the season for the Seashore Twilight Baseball League was held at the home of Norman "Bees" Reeves, and in golf, the Knights of Columbus handed the Mays Landing Union League team its first defeat of the season on the Brigantine course by a score of 25-11.

Night fishing from the Inlet cost only a dollar, including lines and bait! And motorists may recall seeing our first parking meters which went into operation on August 2.

A federal slum clearance project, Baltic to Adriatic, and Kentucky to Illinois Avenues was dedicated in May for 287 families. It is known as Stanley Holmes Village. And Columbus Plaza was officially dedicated on October 12, then observed as Columbus Day. The site was once the farm of Jeremiah Leeds, Absecon Island's first permanent settler.

The three-day Washington's Birthday holiday that year was marked by capacity business! Temperatures ranged in the 50's, and the station master at the P-R-S-L station reported that it required 155 parlor cars to transport the crowds out of town!

The 2:30 train for New York City left in two sections; the 4:10 in seven sections, and the 5:45 in five sections! And there were three trains to Philadelphia as well. The famed "Blue Comet" made two trips out, at 5:35 and 6:35 P.M. Endless lines of cars streamed over the two boulevards homeward bound and buses left every few minutes.

Some of the radio shows we enjoyed on our new Superheterodyne included soap operas such as "The Romance of Helen Trent", "Pepper Young's Family", "Just Plain Bill", and "Ma Perkins". And dramas on "Lux Radio Theatre" and "Big Town".

Songs we heard on those same radios were: "A Foggy Day In London Town", "My Funny Valentine", "The Lady Is A Tramp", "Boo Hoo" and "Thanks For The Memory".

1938

Area employers were paying at least 40¢ an hour, the minimum wage set by the Fair Labor Standards Act of 1938! But jobs were not easy to find, as Atlantic City battled its way out of the Depression.

A savage Atlantic storm washed out the Atlantic City end of the old Brigantine bridge in September and it wasn't until December that the span was reopened to traffic!

Our Fire Prevention Bureau was organized by city ordinance on December 1st. The new ordinance provided for inspectors who daily cover the city in their work. The bureau has been credited with having cut possible fire losses by more than 50% by their diligent prevention efforts!

1938 marked the pinnacle of success in the so-called "Golden Age" of the big bands and many of them were appearing at our hotels, night clubs and piers. Benny Goodman's Orchestra was earning between $8,500 and $10,000 per week. Tommy Dorsey was in the $7,500 class, while Guy Lombardo and Eddy Duchin could command $8,500 a week.

Two of the nation's top swing bands played Atlantic City that season: Jan Savitt and the Top Hatters in the Ballroom of States on Million Dollar Pier, and the great Bunny Berigan in the Marine Ballroom of Steel Pier.

An excerpt from a "Letters To The Editor" column in the old "Daily World" that February reads, "What Atlantic City needs is attractions. Races in May and October will be the greatest. Conventions, of course, are your backbone but see what racing did for Long Branch, and when it left, it ruined the place."

Many of our readers will recall what happened in October, 1938, when Orson Welles' Halloween broadcast of "War Of The Worlds" on the Mercury Theatre over CBS, threw the nation into panic! So realistic was the production that those who had failed to hear the opening of the show thought we really were being invaded by creatures from outer space! Rex Matlack, a former employee of station WPG, which had carried the program, told me their telephone switchboard remained jammed for more than two hours after the program left the air!

It was a good year for motion pictures, and showing on local screens were "Little Miss Broadway", starring Shirley Temple; "Test Pilot", with Clark Gable, Myrna Loy and Spencer Tracy; and "The Adventures of Robin Hood", with that swashbuckling star, Errol Flynn. Most movie houses charged 35¢ for adults and 15¢ for children and we got to see a newsreel, a comedy, "Coming Attractions", of course, plus the feature, all for "one low admission".

And remember these songs from '38? "I'll Be Seeing You", "And The Angels Sing", "You Go To My Head", "My Reverie", and "Change Partners". And we had our share of crazy novelty tunes too, including "The Flat Foot Floogie" (with the Floy, Floy) and "Ferdinand The Bull".

1939

On July 4th, with a banner crowd in town, an entire block of Boardwalk between Missouri Avenue and Columbia Place, went up in flames, destroyed by a fire, which broke out at 7:30 A.M. Many buildings, along with the season's hoped-for profits, were lost including a playland, a shooting gallery, a novelty shop, Bradley's Salt Water Taffy store, a Keno game, "Flicker Follies", a movie house, a waffle shop, Tompkin's Ice Cream Parlor, and Pennyland. Damage was set at more than $105,000!

Atlantic City hotels were adopting a policy of hiring only local residents, with Mayor Charles D. White backing the idea a hundred percent. "Local Jobs For Local Residents" was the slogan and apparently the idea worked, creating additional employment for our own people.

We enjoyed Midget Auto Racing at Convention Hall, which advertised 5,000 seats at 40¢. Racing great Johnny Moretti was directing the events, and he was well-qualified, having driven at Langhorne and Indianapolis! Young Eddie League, Jr. won the annual Marbles Tournament for the second consecutive year. Eddie represented Holy Spirit Grammar School.

Edison Hedges, the local speedboat racer, suffered burns when his 91 cubic inch hydroplane, "Flying Eagle" caught fire during a test run.

Remember a softball team called "Dox Folly"? It was very popular at that time, in the city's Twilight League.

Again, the summer season ushered in many of the top names from the world of entertainment: Steel Pier featured Rudy Vallee and His Connecticut Yankees, Bob Crosby and the Bobcats, singing star Marion Talley, Hal Kemp and His Orchestra, and movie star Arthur Treacher! Down the beach a way, Hamid's Million Dollar Pier spotlighted Rudolf Friml, Jr. and His Concert Orchestra in the Hippodrome, Little Jack Little and His Orchestra in the Ballroom, and the famous Clyde Beatty Circus outdoors!

Made by E. C. Kropp Co., Milwaukee, Wis. Atlantic City Rep. H. S. Sampliner, (JIY).

Pub. by H. S. Sampliner, Atlantic City, N. J. Natural Color Post Card Made in U.S.A. by E. C. Kropp Co., Milwaukee, Wis.

Lucky Teeter and his Hell Drivers put on a show which featured automobiles crashing, rolling over and sailing through the air, inside Convention Hall. We paid 50¢ to watch from the edge of our seats!

In a surprise move, ice cream vendors were banned from the beach that summer, and not even our war veterans were exempted. The edict followed complaints by merchants of unfair competition and lack of sanitation. People were paying $6.25 a ton for coal at the Scranton Coal Company on Bacharach Boulevard.

The city-owned radio station, WPG, decided to call it quits, and its clear-channel frequency of 1100 k.c. went to New York's WNEW. The station had spawned many top personalities, among whom were John Reed King, Ethel Rattay and Norman Brokenshire, whose familiar "How do you do, ladies and gentlemen, how do you do?" became well-known. WPG stood for "World's Play Ground". It went on the air in 1925, but had never been a real money-maker.

There was dancing in the new "Stratosphere Room" of the Traymore, which opened that July, with music by Bill Madden's Orchestra. And on Heinz Pier, singer-organist Lois Miller performed for thousands each evening with her open-air concerts and sing-alongs.

LOIS MILLER .. SINGING ORGANIST..
HEINZ OCEAN PIER

Courtesy H. J. Heinz Co., Pittsburgh, Pa.

87

And this was the year we heard for the first time such songs as "Deep Purple", "If I Didn't Care", "God Bless America", "In The Mood" and "Hold Tight, Hold Tight", (Want Some Seafood, Mama) a really big hit for The Andrews Sisters.

From May til September our nightclubs enjoyed good business, whether they were booking top names or those who had only a local following. Some of those nightspots included the Bath and Turf, the Torch Club, Paddock International, Club Madrid, Erin's Isle Cafe, Clicquot Club, Emerald Cafe and Babette's.

BABETTE'S — MISSISSIPPI AND PACIFIC AVENUES. ATLANTIC CITY. N. J.

Designed and Produced by Harry H. Baumann, 216 W. 18th Street, New York.

1940

An Atlantic City event which brought out the minks, sables, white ties and tails, sleek limousines and countless well-known personages to the Apollo Theatre on January 25th, was the premier of the motion picture "Gone With The Wind"! Mayor C. D. White presented the key to the city to Miss Linda Lackie, who bore a striking resemblance to the film's Scarlett O'Hara, Vivien Leigh.

Other current screen offerings included "Drums Along The Mohawk", "Road To Singapore", with Crosby, Hope and Lamour, and "40 Little Mothers", starring Eddie Cantor, old "Banjo Eyes"!

At Babette's, on Pacific Avenue opposite Convention Hall, Earl Lindsay's "All American Revue" was packin 'em in! Remember its unique bar in the form of a real boat?

Ozzie Nelson and His Orchestra "with vocals by the maestro and lovely Harriet Hilliard" played Hamid's Million Dollar Pier, while Jack Benny and Dennis Day were starring on Steel Pier! Baseball's famed "Sultan of Swat", Babe Ruth, was vacationing here and drawing autograph seekers wherever he went. Noted radio commentator Boake Carter, the "Old Night Owl" was guest speaker at a luncheon of the

Kiwanis Club, and in politics, Frank S. "Hap" Farley defeated Emerson Richards for state Senate.

The cost of food was low compared to today, but then, so were wages, if we had a job! Ham sold for 13¢ a pound, tomatoes were a nickel a pound; and soft drinks were six bottles for a quarter. There was a two-cent deposit on each one, however, in that era before throw-aways. On Saturdays, children made their rounds pulling express wagons, collecting the bottles and turning them in for the deposits! As I recall, the quart sized ones fetched a nickel!

Six persons died and 11 were injured when the two 20,000 gallon water tanks atop the Florida Bathhouse on the Boardwalk at Florida Avenue, crashed through the roof when girders supporting them gave way!

The first "Streamliner" trolleys went into service and were lauded as a big improvement over the old style streetcars, which had been a familiar sight on the streets of Atlantic City for many a year. Now even those streamliners have been relegated to the junkyard and live only in the memories of those of us who rode those swaying conveyances!

In July of 1940, Radio Station WFPG, now WIIN, went on the air at 1420 on the dial with a power of 250 watts. The station had no network affiliation at that time. It later became part of the old Red and Blue Networks, eventually joining the American Broadcasting Company, and in 1951, CBS. The station was owned by The Neptune Broadcasting Corporation, comprised of a number of well-known local businessmen. Only two are known to be living today: Adrian Phillips and Charles Harp. Now we could boast two stations, with WBAB, owned and operated by the Press-Union Publishing Company, having begun operations the preceding January.

Some of the personalities in the early days of WFPG included George Thomas, Bill Campbell, Jim Grohman, Ralf Brent, Mil March, Ed Sweet, also known as Eddie Allen, Bob Brown and Hal Tunis. I joined the staff of WFPG in 1946. The call letters were changed to WIIN in 1978.

Popular voices on WBAB, 1490 on your dial, included those of Ralph Shoemaker, Bern Penrose, Harry Lee, Bob Leach, Bernard Averback, and Dick Hertz.

A lovely 19-year old Philadelphia brunette, Frances Burke, was the reigning Miss America, and Thomas D. Taggart, known locally as "Two Gun Tommy" was the colorful Mayor of Atlantic City.

A unique attraction for visitors and residents then was a program of physical fitness exercises conducted on the Virginia Avenue beach by Albert Lyneer, a graduate of Temple University and former Athletic Director of the Ventnor City Beach Patrol. Lyneer had quite a following and folks gathered long before the 8:45 A.M. start of the exercises. There was no charge and it was lots of fun for old and young alike!

Another unusual attraction, one which closed that September, was the Beech-Nut Circus on Central Pier, billed as "The Biggest Little Show On Earth". Ralph Glenn was manager of the Circus, which contained three rings, a stage and a moving parade of floats with performing acrobats, clowns, horses, elephants and more, all electrically operated. Let's hope that somewhere, that mechanical marvel survives today so it may one day enchant the young and young-at-heart of future generations.

1940 saw a whole new batch of great songs: "Fools Rush In", "Only Forever", "The Breeze And I", "All Or Nothing At All", and "Three Little Fishies" (In A Itty Bitty Pool).

1941

The summer of '41 . . . one last fling before Pearl Harbor and our entry into World War II, but we didn't know it at the time! As they had done for almost a hundred years, thousands upon thousands of visitors converged on Atlantic City for relaxation and pleasure! The big bands were in their heyday, and booked into the Million Dollar Pier that summer were the orchestras of Vaughn Monroe, Tony Pastor, Hal McIntyre, Van Alexander, Charlie Spivak and Will Bradley.

In June, George White's "Scandals" played that pier, and screen actor Victor McLaglen, in person, was booked during the same month. On the screen was "The Singing Hills", starring Gene Autry and Smiley Burnette.

The crack train "Blue Comet" which ran between Atlantic City and New York (actually Jersey City) between 1929 and 1941. The train became a legend in its own time, a period spanning only 12 years. Photo from the collection of H. Gerald MacDonald.

The famed "Blue Comet", long the last word in deluxe rail travel, made its final run on Sunday, September 28, 1941. It had gone into service on the old Jersey Central Railroad out of the Reading station, Arkansas and Atlantic Avenues here, making its inaugural run to Jersey City on February 21, 1929. That train was really a sight to see as it sped along the shining rails! And for those of us who remember its unusual whistle, the Blue Comet will never be gone!

Some of our readers may recall a mongrel dog named "Rags" who helped his master, Patrolman Anthony Myura, on traffic duty at Arkansas and Arctic Avenues. "Rags", it is said, died of a broken heart at the age of 13 when he was retired and kept at home because of his advancing years. In 1941, Mayor Taggart dedicated a plaque to "Rags" at the Union Terminal Building at the intersection where the faithful dog had worked.

Jonathon Pitney Village, with 331 units, was dedicated April 1st. Local markets were selling coffee for 15¢ a pound, lettuce for a nickel a head, cream cheese 23¢ a pound, tomato soup for 5¢ a can, oranges for 15¢ a dozen, fresh porgies at 9¢ a pound, and flour at 45¢ for a 12-pound bag! Our population count had dropped to 64,000!

With war raging in Europe and America hoping it would be able to escape involvement, we continued our peaceful endeavors and danced to such tunes as "Tuxedo Junction", "Blues In The Night", "A Nightingale Sang In Berkeley Square", "Blueberry Hill", and "Amapola".

Later in the year, another song became popular for obvious reasons. It was entitled "We Did It Before And We Can Do It Again"! War was declared after our Naval Base at Pearl Harbor, Hawaii, was attacked by the Imperial Japanese Navy on December 7, a day which then President Franklin Delano Roosevelt stated would "live in infamy".

If you're in your mid-fifties or thereabouts, you don't need much prodding to recall where you were and what you were doing that day! I was enjoying a movie at the old Hollywood Theatre, here in Atlantic City, and when we came out, a newsboy was shouting the news of the attack, news which could change my life and the lives of millions of people around the world!

Of local interest in 1941 was the marriage of Enoch L. "Nucky" Johnson and Florence "Flossie" Osbeck on July 31st, at the First Presbyterian Church, Pacific and Pennsylvania Avenues. The wedding was a closed affair with ony about 70 invited guests. Three members of Atlantic City's Police Department stood guard. They were Sergeant Joseph Lodovico, Captain Harry Saunders and Patrolman Roy Smith. A gala reception followed at Johnson's Spanish-style cottage on Iowa Avenue!

Within a few hours, "Nucky" would go before a federal judge to hear pronouncement of a sentence which slammed shut prison doors on the long-time Republican leader of Atlantic County! He had been found guilty of income tax evasion on two counts. "Nuck's" departure was cheered by some, and lamented by many, for it has been said that he never refused help to anyone in need.

1942

The words "dim-out" are today just a memory for those who lived during the period when the ruling was in effect and mean nothing at all to younger people who weren't around Atlantic City during World War II. Following a directive from military authorities, all lights along our boardwalk and in windows and signs facing the ocean, were to be extinguished or dimmed because of the proximity of enemy ships.

The dim-out officially began March 19, 1942. Shades were installed at all windows, and awnings were kept down over shops on the board-walk. On August 18, the face of City Hall clock at Tennessee and Atlantic Avenues was darkened and not turned on again til 1945. By May of '42, all illumination in store windows was cut down to 30%. And in March of the following year, full dim-out regulations went into effect with all outdoor lighting, including street lamps, shielded to prevent any upward glow. At that time, reports had it that Axis nation vessels were lurking off our coast within a short distance of our beaches!

The Atlantic City Airport, located on a 5,500-acre tract at English Creek and Pomona Roads, at Tilton Road in Pomona, was leased to the U.S. Navy in October. The lease agreement was extended to the duration of the war, plus six months with improvements scheduled, which would cost $6,000,000! At the peak of its operation during and following the war, the U.S. Naval Air Station, Pomona, was one of the largest and most strategic installations on the Atlantic seaboard! Today it is known as The Federal Aviation Administration Technical Center . Adjacent to the main installation, the Atlantic City Airport continues to play an important role in the transportation picture here, being capable of handling much larger planes than Bader Field, which is the smaller airport just a few blocks from our boardwalk.

The "Handbook of Atlantic City" for 1942, printed by the Amusement Publishing Company, lists our town as being "within an overnight train ride of 60% of the total population of the United States". Our population then was listed at 65,748. The ice hockey season for the famed Atlantic City Seagulls, ran from mid-November to March 21st, with Friday and Saturday night games at Convention Hall. They were quite a team and many local sports enthusiasts still recall with pride, the days when we had our own hockey team.

Conventions held here in 1942 included the Progressive Education Association, National Association of Hosiery Manufacturers, The American Medical Association, American Gas Association, The New Jersey Educators' Association and The National Council of English Teachers. Charles Harp was President of the Chamber of Commerce.

The nearby Brigantine Golf and Country Club was offering year 'round play with greens fees of 75¢ daily and a dollar on Saturdays, Sundays and holidays!

Best picture of the year was "Mrs. Miniver", which starred Walter Pigeon, Greer Garson and Henry Wilcoxon. Songs of 1942 included "Paper Doll", "Time Was", "The Things I Love", "Walkin' By The River", and that hand-clapping melody, "Deep In The Heart Of Texas".

In addition to these, we had many songs which reflected our feelings and longings for loved ones away in the service: "Dearly Beloved", "He Wears A Pair Of Silver Wings", "This Is Worth Fighting For", "I Left My Heart At The Stage Door Canteen", and "When The Lights Go On Again All Over The World".

1943

The Chalfonte-Haddon Hall Hotels were closed to the general

public beginning in August, as England General Hospital, one of the Army's largest such facilities during World War II, opened in that boardwalk hostelry. A temporary bridge between the two hotels was built at about that time, but was later removed.

England General was named for Lt. Col. Thomas M. England who died that year. He had been a member of the Army Medical Corps since the days of the Spanish-American War, during which he spent 20 nights in the bed of a yellow fever victim so that he might learn enough about the disease to treat it successfully and perhaps help to wipe it out!

Atlantic City's Fire Department had 320 volunteers, serving without pay, in the Fire Reserves organized to combat possible bomb fires or others which the paid firefighters might not be able to handle due to other calls. Joseph Hackney and Lester Jackson were in charge of that valuable arm of our Fire Department.

The movie "Casablanca" won the Oscar for best motion picture. Other screen fare of '43 included "Bataan", with Robert Taylor, at the Cinema, Ohio and Atlantic, "Coney Island", starring Betty Grable, at the Embassy, Atlantic and New York Avenues, "White Savage", with John Hall and Sabu, at the Lyric, Atlantic and Florida Avenues, and "Cat People", starring Simone Simon, at the Palace, Mississippi and Atlantic. Admission at those last two theatres was "10¢ for all til 2 p.m., servicemen: 10¢ at all times".

The U. S. Coast Guard Training Station on South Virginia Avenue had 18 "Spars" and expected many more. They were the distaff side of that branch of the service. A restaurant ran an ad in the local "Press" seeking a salad man for $30 for a six-day week! The Atlantic City and Shore Railroad, which operated street cars on Atlantic Avenue, said July business was up between 35% and 40% over the previous July.

The new lapel insignia for honorably discharged veterans was introduced. It eventually became affectionately known as "The Ruptured Duck". Many local servicemen were being decorated for bravery in the line of duty, while the papers carried news of many a man who would never come home.

The ratio of women donating blood destined for servicemen overseas was 10 to one over men! One such woman, Mrs. Michael Ruane, was the mother of five servicemen! While the Chalfonte Haddon Hall had been taken over for service as a hospital, the St. Charles and the Claridge were re-opened to the public that year, following 12 months of Army occupation. Colonel E. R. Householder was commanding officer of the Atlantic City Basic Training Center.

Roy Shinn was Chief Air Raid Warden here and no cameras or binoculars were permitted on the beach or boardwalk for the duration! You could have bought an 8-room house on Tallahassee Avenue for $6,000, and a six-room home on Caspian Avenue for $2,500!

Motoring to seashore resorts had been curtailed by government regulations and Frank P. Gravatt, President of the Amusement Men's Association of Atlantic City, led a fight to have the order rescinded because it was hurting business. It was a ban on "one-day recreational driving" which did keep many visitors away. The Office of Defense

Transportation ordered public service coordinated transport to cut mileage of its buses by 95,000 miles a week to conserve gasoline, but Atlantic City was not included in the cutback.

Hamid's Pier that summer had its usual parade of name bands including Johnny Long, Mal Hallett and Gracie Barry and Her Orchestra. And remember those great Jitterburg Jamborees with cash prizes?

At Steel Pier, Sammy Kaye was in for a week, followed by Bobby Sherwood and His Band, Guy Lombardo and His Orchestra and Will Osborne and His "Slide Music". And let's not forget the antics of "Sharkey", the trained seal!

In spite of the war and its accompanying sadness, people somehow continued to sing and dance to the new crop of songs: "Brazil", "Pistol Packin' Mama", "A Lovely Way To Spend An Evening", "People Will Say We're In Love" and the novelty tune "Mairzy Doats And Dozey Doats". And songsmiths continued to turn out war songs such as "Comin' In On A Wing And Prayer", "Don't Sit Under The Apple Tree", "What Do You Do In The Infantry?", "Goodbye Sue", and "Praise The Lord And Pass The Ammunition."

1944

"The Worst Storm In 40 Years"! That's how the Weather Bureau described the devastating hurricane of September 14, 1944, in Atlantic City. I own an electrical transcription which is a type of recording used by radio stations until about 1955. On that disc, the voice of Ed Allen, also known as Ed Sweet, describes the effects of the storm to a nationwide audience on the old Blue Network of the National Broadcasting Company. In the background can be heard the roar of the surf and the howling of the wind! And by that time, the worst was over!

Ed was working from an open window in the main control room of Station WFPG on the evening the hurricane struck! He tells of several street cars of the old Shore Fast Line stranded on Virginia Avenue with water up to floor level! Civil Defense workers had to wade through deep water and the Inlet section was inaccessible except by boat, and even that wasn't easy!

All area physicians had been summoned to duty, including those military doctors attached to England General Hospital, due to the many injuries incurred by victims of the big blow. When Sweet's broadcast was made at 7 P.M. Eastern War Time, on September 14, he remarked that property damage alone was already estimated at more than $2,000,000! Winds of 65 and 70 miles an hour had uprooted trees, destroyed signs and knocked out huge plate glass shop windows. A woman had been blown from a roof by the force of the wind and was in serious condition!

Power failed in the city at 5:27 P.M. so the broadcast to which we refer was made by using battery-operated equipment and a special phone line to Philadelphia's WFIL. And, oh yes . . . a flashlight! The hurricane had hit the city at approximately 3 P.M. and lasted about two hours but that's all it took to wreak havoc and destruction throughout Absecon Island! An official tally later set damage at a staggering $4,500,000!

During the years between 1897 and 1944, visitors and residents were fascinated by the creations of the talented sand artists who worked on our beaches. Using ordinary sand held together by what is understood to have been a so-called "secret substance", they fashioned all manner of interesting objects: animals, fish, autos, buildings, historical scenes, people, and whatever the passersby requested. These artists subsisted on the coins tossed down to them by boardwalk promenaders. Philip McCord is said to have been the very first sand artist in Atlantic City. The practice was abolished by City Commision following the hurricane of 1944.

Popular radio shows included "Valiant Lady", "Stella Dallas", "Ethel and Albert", "Hop Harrigan", "Easy Aces", and "The Frank Sinatra Show". Some of 1944's hit songs include "Amor", "Twilight Time", "Candy", "Saturday Night Is The Loneliest Night In The Week", and "Sentimental Journey".

1945

The world famed Heinz Pier, at Massachusetts Avenue and the beach, failed to open for the season of 1945! It had been so severly damaged in the hurricane the year before that it was decided to tear it down. Originally "Iron Pier", the structure was the first pier in our city to be erected on iron pilings!

After the Heinz Company of Pittsburgh purchased the pier in 1898, they enlarged it and established a complete exhibit featuring its famous "57 Varieties" and passed out free samples of its products and a little pickle pin as a souvenir. Perhaps you have one among those old mementoes. I still have mine!

HEINZ PIER, ATLANTIC CITY, N. J.

No Publisher listed.

It was the height of hostilies during World War II and Army occupation of Atlantic City jammed almost 50 of our hotels and more than half a million service personnel underwent basic training here for various branches of our Armed Forces. Remember the ranks of hundreds of uniformed people marching in cadence along our boardwalk to and from the hotels which served as their barracks? In 1945, the U.S. Army paid the city $500,000 for use, maintenance and necessary repairs to Convention Hall, which had been used by the Air Force for offices and training purposes from July 15, 1952 until 1945.

Our Mayor was Joseph Altman, a prominent attorney and former athlete who had taken office in 1944. Altman has been credited with introducing many innovations in city government and being instrumental in the progress of our city during his long tenure. He retired in 1967.

The really big stories of the year were, of course, V-E Day in May and V-J Day in September! The war was over, with Germany laying down its arms first, to be followed 118 days later by Japan. Hundreds of Atlantic Citians made ready to come home and start over, but for many others, the war had ended earlier, in injury or death.

The year's best motion picture was "Lost Weekend", starring Ray Milland on a five-day alchoholic binge! Two more great films were "A Tree Grows In Brooklyn", with James Dunn, and "National Velvet", which featured a 12-year old who was to continue her rise to fame in the movies, Elizabeth Taylor.

Some of the year's top tunes were "Cruising Down The River", "It Might As Well Be Spring", "Laura", "Let It Snow, Let It Snow", and "June Is Bustin' Out All Over".

1946

Early in the year, Mayor Altman forecast the greatest period of prosperity in Atlantic City's history! The Mayor cited figures of record-breaking convention bookings for 1946-47, and gave the city an even chance of becoming the U. N. capital! That was in reference to a visit by seven men who came to the resort that winter to look over our town as a possible site for the United Nations building!

The Bayless Pharmacy and Warner Hotel were gutted by a $200,000 fire. In January, the Absecon Boulevard was closed after a tanker crashed into a temporary wooden bridge. Sun Oil's "Raritan Sun" had hit the span, causing the re-routing of all traffic to Albany Avenue Boulevard. The Ole Hansen Company was the contractor for the new $1,187,000 six-lane bridge which was to replace the temporary span.

Ventnorites got a surprise when 2,000 bottles washed ashore near Buffalo Avenue, creating quite a mystery! The labels were missing and the contents looked, smelled and felt like shampoo, but so far as we know, the source of the bottles was never established.

A temporary budget of $2,030,000 was fixed for Atlantic City and some municipal employees were in line for bonuses. For families with loved ones in uniform, there was good news almost every day as troop ships arrived in port with returning veterans.

The beautiful new Atlantic City Race Course in McKee City opened on July 22, and the names of Bob Hope and Frank Sinatra, plus those of six nationally known band leaders, were on the list of stockholders in the new enterprise. They were Kay Kyser, Harry James, Sammy Kaye, Xavier Cugat, Phil Spitalny and Axel Stordahl.

Wrestling at Convention Hall featured Dave Levin vs. The Golden Angel. Admission was 75¢ and $1.50. Lawley Motor Company on North Iowa Avenue was the place to go to see the exciting new Nash automobile.

The Boardwalk National Bank's Statement of Condition showed cash in reserve in the amount of $8,256,000. Other assets brought the total to $39,525,000. The reigning Miss America was 21-year-old Marilyn Buford, of Los Angeles, California. Color television was being promised by broadcast engineers in 1946, even though black-and-white TV still was in the experimental stages.

Amphibious plane service between Atlantic City and other shore points was being considered but delivery of equipment was a problem. Six trolley cars were purchased by the local transportation company from the city of Fort Wayne, Indiana. They were reconditioned and used on the Atlantic Avenue run during peak hours. It was impossible, at the time, to buy new rolling stock due to the shortage of metal following the war.

On the local real estate scene, a 28-room hotel on North Virginia Avenue, with two stores, was on the market at $12,000! If you think that was a bargain, how about this? Three adjoining bungalow-style homes in Margate at 8200, 8202 and 8204 Atlantic Avenue were for sale at $15,000! For all three!

Coal was in short supply in those first few months following the end of hostilities and several city departments combined forces to cut and deliver free firewood to families unable to obtain other fuel. Deliveries were made by city-owned trucks.

If you were a movie fan, you may have visited the Embassy to see Fred Astaire and Lucille Bremmer in "Yolanda and the Thief", or the Apollo to see "They Were Expendable", with Robert Montgomery and John Wayne. The Alan, Kentucky and Arctic Avenues, was showing "Captain Kidd", with Charles Laughton and Randolph Scott, while the Capital was showing "What Next, Corporal Hargrove?".

Some of 1946's big network radio shows were Don McNeill's Breakfast Club, Grand Central Station, Life of Riley, Truth or Consequences, 20 Questions, Your Hit Parade, John J. Anthony and Grand Ole Opry.

1947

A city ordinance was adopted on the 15th of May and approved by public referendum in June, whereby a luxury tax would be levied on such items as alcoholic beverages, tobacco, admissions to amusements and room rentals. Originally introduced under a state act in 1945 and becoming law without the signature of the Governor, the bill was fought in the courts and ruled unconstitutional in 1946.

However, with the adoption of the new city ordinance the following year and approval by referendum, the controversial tax went into effect and continues to this day, although at this writing it is being phased out. It is unique to Atlantic City and, so far as we can learn, there is no such tax anywhere in the nation! It collects five cents on the dollar and is in lieu of a state sales tax on the items covered. Monies collected remain in Atlantic City rather than being transferred to the state treasury.

Remember the good times at the old Hygeia Pool, Rhode Island Avenue and the Boardwalk? It was quite a place! The pool was built in 1910 and provided healthful fun for thousands of persons. It was dismantled in 1947. The Hygeia was not the first indoor pool in the resort. That honor goes to a pool opened at Ocean Avenue and the 'Walk in 1891. The following year, another was opened at Virginia Avenue and the Boardwalk by George W. Jackson, who later headed the Steel Pier Company.

But getting back to the Hygeia, it was a huge pool and boasted clear, clean water at all times. A nominal charge was made and it was well worth it! People met at the pool regularly and it was for years, "the" place to enjoy healthful exercise.

Other early day pools in Atlantic City included that at the old Brighton Casino, the Park Ocean Parlor and Baths, the Ambassador Hotel pool, built in 1920, and the President Hotel pool, constructed about 1926.

Pub. by the Sithens Post Card Co., Atlantic City, N. J.

It was a great year for beautiful songs, among which were: "Ballerina", a big hit for singing star Vaughn Monroe, "Dream, Dream, Dream", "Tenderly", "Smoke, Smoke, Smoke That Cigarette", and "Near You", which made pianist Francis Craig a star almost overnight.

Singer Connee Boswell played Steel Pier and so did "the man who played the sweetest trumpet in the world", Charlie Spivak. The Emergency Erosion Committee was urging voters to okay the luxury tax pointing to the need for money to replenish our beaches. The vote, on June 3, was almost two-to-one in favor!

You may have bought your new Packard that year from MacMullin on Arctic Avenue, or your new Willys at Arthur Motors on Atlantic

Avenue. "Koons Lucky Money" was a popular radio show on WFPG, and many persons refused to leave the house for fear of missing a telephone call from Bob Brown or me, giving them the opportunity to win the jackpot! It was sponsored by Koons' Jewelry Store, Illinois and Atlantic Avenues.

There was plenty of night life with Dolph Traymon and His Orchestra in the Holiday Room of the Mayflower, on the Boardwalk at Tennessee Avenue, Pupi Campo at the Chelsea Hotel, Steve Gibson and the Redcaps at the Club Nomad, and Larry Steele's "Smart Affairs of 1948" at the Club Harlem. An added attraction was Roy "Little Jazz" Eldredge, in person! Other favorite gathering places for after-hours afficionados were Dusty Roads, at Mississippi and Atlantic, and Don Riddle's Harbor Bar, on North New Hampshire Avenue.

The owners of the Brighton Hotel paid more than $1,000,000 for a piece of property with a 200-foot boardwalk frontage, including more than half a dozen smart shops.

Chilton Printing Co., Philadelphia, Pa.

1948

The Atlantic City Fire Department staged some great minstrel shows in the late 40's, on Steel Pier, and they were usually sold out affairs! In 1948 the show was held on November 26, 27 and 28th, three big nights, with Edward Mulvihill as Director and Lester Jackson as Interlocutor. End men included Billy Mitchell, John Reilly, Raymond Cranston, John McNally, Frank Caffery and Joe Smith. Music was by Bert Estlow's Orchestra. Among the soloists were LeRoy Camp, Rod Jordan, Filbert Rowley, Leon Leopardi, Rod Lewallen and Anthony Campanella. Joe Hackney was Stage Manager.

Some of the songs which probably were featured during those 1948 performances of the A.C.F.D. Minstrels were: "We Could Make Such Beautiful Music Together", "Beg Your Pardon", "I Still Get

Jealous'', "Papa, Won't You Dance With Me?'', "You Were Only Fooling'' (While I Was Falling In Love), and "My Happiness'', as well as many of the old standards so popular with minstrel shows.

Those productions were put on for three years: 1947, 1948 and 1949, after which they were discontinued.

You may have been among the huge throng gathered for the dedication ceremonies when the Atlantic City Municipal Stadium at Bader Field opened on October 22, 1948. It cost $350,000. Plans were already being made to celebrate the resort's 100th birthday, coming up in 1954, and a group met for the first time to lay the groundwork.

The late historian and inventor, Erwin Schwatt was its chairman. Initial plans called for a gala year-long celebration involving residents, past and present, and the business community as well. And yes, our visitors were welcome, too, with their presence and ideas.

1948 saw the last of the Shore Fast Line trolleys, when the final run was made on January 18, with snow on the ground, and an aura of sadness pervading each car. That sadness was passed on between the motorman and the passengers whose thoughts raced back across the years, recalling happier times on that famous line.

Many a courtship had taken place on those conveyances! One local woman has related how her boyfriend would board the car on the mainland at one stop, while she got on at another. They would travel separately to the boardwalk in Atlantic City, but return home together. Imagine their surprise one evening when they were greeted by some friends they thought they'd been fooling! She says the secret was out, and they could do nothing about it but laugh it off!

Buses took over all runs from then on. They were faster, smoother-riding and more dependable, but there was something special about a ride on one of those old, swaying Shore Fast Line trolleys! They'd been cursed and blessed, and now they were gone.

In sports that year, Ray Dooney, former Atlantic City High School grid star, scored two touchdowns and passed for a third as his University of Pennsylvania football team lost to undefeated Army by a score of 21 to 19.

The famous Tucker automobile, which was far ahead of its time, was creating a mild sensation displayed on a huge revolving turntable on Hamid's Million Dollar Pier! A beautiful machine, with many innovations which would not appear on production cars for years, the Tucker's most unusual feature was a cyclops-style headlamp mounted between the two conventional ones!!! The car never got into mass production and only a very few were made.

1949

Hundreds, perhaps thousands, of unusual events have taken place in Atlantic City. One such happening was the underwater wedding performed inside the Steel Pier's Diving Bell 30 feet below the surface of the ocean, on August 22. Miss Ruth Ehlers, then 17 and Louis Villani, 21, both of North Bergen, New Jersey, were joined in holy wedlock by the Reverend

Shore Fast Line Trolley, Virginia Avenue and the Boardwalk. The line operated between Atlantic City and Ocean City including the Shore Road communities on the Mainland between 1906 and 1948. From the collection of M.E. Borgnis.

John R. Vann, of New York City.

The Diving Bell, with its operator, Barton Bach, remained underwater for 14 minutes before popping to the surface. When it did, Mr. and Mrs. Villani were the first people to have been married underwater, according to records of the time. Little Vicki Gold, daughter of our city's official photographer, Al Gold, served as flower girl.

In 1949, we rode the trolley from the Inlet all the way to the end of the Island at Longport, for a ten-cent fare! Popular dining places in town, which are now just memories, include Sid Hartfield's, Heilig's, Alfred's, Babette's, Jimmy's Albemarle, Kent's, The Senator Hotel Grille, The Stanley, Mammy's, Tides Tavern, DiLullo's, The Far East, and The Original Kornblau's. Many's the delicious sandwich I packed away at Kornblau's. And the Stanley was a popular gathering place for those working odd hours, and that included me, since I got off the air at WFPG when we signed off at 1:05 A.M.

Tichnor Quality Views. Made only by Tichnor Bros., Inc., Boston, Mass.

Outdoor sports we enjoyed here way back then, were sailing from the Inlet docks, deep sea fishing, bicycling on the 'walk, only til 9 A.M. in those days, golfing, gunning, trapshooting, horseback riding on the beach, October thru May, rolling chair rides, tennis at the Ventnor City courts, and those popular bus trips to the Mainland communities and Ocean City from the terminal at Virginia Avenue and the boardwalk.

Sports enthusiasts cheered the opening of the John Henry "Pop" Lloyd Stadium at Absecon Boulevard and Huron Avenue. The facility is named for the local black athlete who has been described by sports writers as one of the greatest all-round baseball players in the United States! In 1977, Lloyd was installed posthumously in the Baseball Hall of Fame at Cooperstown, New York. Ray Dooney was named Captain of his University of Pennsylvania football team early in the 1949 season, and later that year was honored by the Press Club of Atlantic City as the citizen who did the most to spread the name and fame of the resort.

That September, the Ballroom of States and other structures on the Million Dollar Pier, Arkansas Avenue and the beach, were destroyed by fire. Damage was great, including the loss of the famous racehorse electric sign, a local landmark for years, which had won and lost many a dollar for people betting on the outcome!

We had only three radio stations in '49: WBAB, WFPG and WMID. Al Owen was a popular disc jockey with WMID and attracted many famous guests to his turntables for interviews. The music which emanated from the studios of those stations had to include such current songs as "Jealous Heart", "She Wore A Yellow Ribbon", "You're Breaking My Heart", "Buttons And Bows", and "Mona Lisa".

1950

As the new decade dawned, Atlantic City's population stood at 61,642. James J. Tynan, street lighting specialist of the Atlantic City Electric Company, reported to Mayor Altman and the City Commission that Christmas lighting on the major streets of the resort and the boardwalk had cost $1,200.

Local movie houses were showing many first-run features including "My Blue Heaven", with Betty Grable and Dan Dailey, at the Apollo; "A Lonely Place", starring Humphrey Bogart, at the Colonial; and "Kiss Tomorrow Goodbye", with James Cagney, at the Stanley.

Popular after-dark spots, no longer in existence, were El Capitan, on the Boardwalk at St. James Place, The 500 Club, 6 South Missouri Avenue, Club Nomad on Bacharach Boulevard and The Dude Ranch, "Way Out West On The 'Walk", at Connecticut Avenue.

Natural Color Post Card Made in U.S.A. by E. C. Kropp Co., Milwaukee, Wis.

The Miss America Pageant "went Hollywood" that year as camera crews descended on the town making background shots for a forthcoming

103

Warner Brothers motion picture. Patricia Freeman, Miss Atlantic City, was official hostess to the visiting beauties.

For the first time in Pageant history, a coast-to-coast broadcast of the finals was beamed via radio from the stage of Convention Hall with the entire show carried by most of the stations of the ABC Radio Network. The originating station was WFPG and I'm proud to have been the announcer for that historic broadcast. That's the year Yolande Betbeze, a 21-year-old brunette, who entered the contest as Miss Alabama, captured the honors.

The Dupont Exhibit was a popular boardwalk attraction, and our hotels continued to report heavy bookings for upcoming conventions. "Dungaree Hops" were drawing the young people to the Jewish Community Center on Virginia Avenue, and Center Director Norman Shamberg and Athletic Director "Uncle Sam" Greenberg said the hops were just one of many social and athletic activities designed to keep the kids occupied.

A brand new home in Chelsea Heights could be purchased for $10,500 in 1950, featuring two bedrooms, kitchen, living room and more, on a large lot! Wonder what it's worth today? F-H-A mortgages cost only 4¼% and if you were an ex-G.I. you could get one at 4%!

Louis Prima, the trumpet star who "Played Pretty for the People" appeared in the Marine Ballroom on Steel Pier that summer. And the big 4th of July weekend saw Danny Kaye, and Her Singing Nibs, Miss Georgia Gibbs, in person on the Music Hall stage!

In September, Thomas D. Taggart, colorful ex-Mayor of Atlantic City who served from 1940 to 1944, passed away suddenly at the age of 49. Police Captain William Mulloy drew the ire of many resort bicyclists when he announced passage of a law requiring every bike to be registered as protection against theft.

Mayor Altman was lobbying for state support for the City Marina. Cost of the project was estimated to be in the neighborhood of $400,000. Sightings of unidentified flying objects were reported in our area that year, but then, as now, they were often dismissed as merely jet airplanes traveling through the air at 20,000 feet!

On November 25, a howling sou'easter hit town, causing such widespread damage that 10,000 claims were filed with insurance companies! Railroad tracks were ripped up on the meadows for almost 2,000 feet and service was disrupted for about two weeks!

The 62-foot trawler "Kristine M.", captained by Morten Mortensen, left her dock here on Thanksgiving Day, November 23, on a six-day fishing trip and was never heard from again! Not one piece of wreckage was found. Ironically, the "Kristine M." was launched during the hurricane of 1944 by Stanley Van Sant and Son, since everything was in readiness for her to leave the ways when the water began to rise. The ship died as she had been born . . . in stormy seas!

Atlantic City's hotels were offering fine entertainment for their guests, as well as the public, with the Lynn Brothers, fronted by Teddy Lee and his spinning bass in the Surf 'N' Sand Room of The Seaside; Bennie Bishop and His Orchestra, with vocalist Lucille Russo was featured in the Olde English Tavern of the Ritz Carlton, and there were Arthur Murray dance exhibitions nightly in the Holiday Room of the Mayflower!

Music has always been a vital part of the history of this resort and 1950 saw such new songs as "Tennessee Waltz", "My Heart Cries For You", "Be My Love", "Daddy's Little Girl", and the tune on which all the gang joined in, "Goodnight Irene".

1951

The U.S. Department of Commerce released figures based on 1948 business which showed the Atlantic City metropolitan area distributing an annual payroll of $12,343,000, and handling a $38,192,000 volume of business! Hotels accounted for the major part of that money, and 341 were listed. The department reported these hotels had a total of 23,450 rooms and a payroll of $12,295,000.

Special policemen on the boardwalk were complaining that they were finding it difficult to enforce the law banning swimsuits there, since it was almost impossible to distinguish swimsuits from sunsuits!

The city's Safety Council was asking the Commission for the return of the Traffic Squad which had been abolished. During the 70 days it had been in force, traffic accidents were down by 99%. The 10¢ beer appeared to be on its way out as the city's beverage men were calling for a uniform 15¢ charge for the amber brew. It had to do with the luxury tax.

The Chamber of Commerce launched a year 'round beautification drive planning to use a series of before and after photos of sites cleared of trash and refuse. The Catalina swimsuit people pulled out of their sponsorship of the Miss America Pageant saying it was teaming up with Pan American World Airways to put on a "Miss Universe" Contest. They said our Pageant had become a talent contest rather than focusing on the body beautiful.

The controversial Hadacol remedy was sweeping the country, and many people in our area swore it helped them! Hadacol was the invention of Senator Dudley LeBlanc, who boasted that his product would relieve your vitamin deficiencies. Sales were listed at 27,000,000 bottles at $1.25 each, for 1950.

Brigantine got dial phones that year, and we paid a nickel for a 12-ounce bottle of Pepsi Cola. Remember their catchy jingle about how it hit the spot? Cramer's Supermarket was advertising the finest steer beef, chuck roast, pork chops or corned beef . . . your choice for 69¢ a pound! And if you shopped in the evening, between 7 and 9, you had a good chance of getting your groceries free, as two lucky shoppers were the winners each week when the bell sounded!

Our hockey team, the Seagulls, returned home after a grueling, road trip on the Eastern Amateur League circuit. Herb Foster was the Coach. The Arctic Avenue Y.M.C.A. won the Interstate Basketball Tournament.

At the movies, Jose Ferrer was starring in "Cyrano DeBergerac" at the Cinema, Bette Davis was in "Payment On Demand", at the Stanley, and Joseph Cotten was featured in "September Affair", at the Warner. Organist Del Zane was the initial attraction at the new Zanzibar Club.

The one and only Pearl Bailey was on stage at the Yacht Club, formerly Babette's, Sophie Tucker was at the 500, and Bobby Roberts and His Orchestra played for dancing when the B'nai B'rith Women of Atlantic City held their annual donor dinner dance in the Embassy Room of the Strand Hotel.

Steel Pier continued to be the highlight of a visit to Atlantic City with such performers as the Mills Brothers, Mary Small, Joan Edwards and the orchestras of Vaughn Monroe, Ralph Flanagan, and Frankie Carle. At the Senator Hotel, capacity crowds were enjoying Monte Proser's La Vie En Rose show, direct from New York.

Rosemary Clooney had two big hits that year with "Come On-A My House" and "Mixed Emotions". Then there were other great songs including "So Long, It's Been Good To Know Yuh", "Sound Off", "The Little White Cloud That Cried", "I Get Ideas" and "Because Of You".

1952

The summer season brought another spectacular attraction to Steel Pier when Ronald Harrison, a 50-year old half-Sioux Indian from Florida was "buried alive" in a six-foot long concrete box for 42 days! The feat established a world's record. Harrison, who was fed through a tube containing his own secret life-sustaining liquid formula, said he was protesting the high cost of living, even at that time, a cause for protest.

I remember seeing crowds gathered around Harrison's "tomb" watching him lying there in repose under a of pane of glass. It was bizarre, but it brought in the people!

The November 7th edition of Charlie Seel's "Atlantic City Reporter" carries a story stating that Director of Public Safety Thomas R. Wootton intended to prove that his department was undermanned and needed beefing up to bring Atlantic City's Police and Fire Departments up to minimum necessary strength!

After 20 years of being on the losing end of presidential elections, Atlantic City and County G-O-P voters jubilantly found themselves with a Republican president! A record number of voters, some 85% of the 79,224 registered, went to the polls to help elect Dwight D. Eisenhower.

January 7 dawned cold and clear in Atlantic City. Early that day, Fred Haggerty, popular "morning man" at radio station WFPG, noticed smoke as he gazed out the studio window on Steel Pier, in the direction of St. Charles Place and the Boardwalk. Before the fire that caused that smoke would be brought under control, many fine old buildings would be leveled, with damage counted in the millions! It was to go down in the annals of the Atlantic City Fire Department as the "St. Charles Place fire" which began in the old Congress Hotel at 7:08 A.M.

The Congress was a six-story frame hotel, formerly the Raleigh, at 170 St. Charles Place. It was closed for the winter and there were no occupants. The owner came to adjust the oil burner and smelled smoke. He ran across the street to the New Davis Hotel but was unable to arouse anyone. He then went to the Lorraine Hotel, next to the Congress, where he phoned in the alarm.

Destroyed in the fire, in addition to the above hotels, were 25 guest houses, and numerous shops and stores, including a rolling chair stand at 717 Boardwalk. Also destroyed by the flames was Engine Company #3's pumper, a 1929 American La France which became the victim of a fire "pincers" situation when the flames from the Congress Hotel and the New Davis met in the center of St. Charles Place!

On January 10, Mayor Altman and Commissioners William S. Cuthbert, Daniel Bader, Phillip Gravatt and William F. Casey ordered a resolution drawn up to convey recognition and commendation to the firefighters, both officers and men, for the heroism they displayed that day!

A most vivid account, together with a number of pictures, is contained in Deputy Chief Franklin Kemp's fine book "Firefighting By The Seashore" from which comes this report.

In sports, Don Gehrmann, the champion trackman from Milwaukee, ran the mile on the boardwalk in four minutes, five-and-three-tenths seconds in May, wearing cross-country running shoes! Ed Stetser and Ed Solitaire swam around Absecon Island to set up the promotion for the late Jim Toomey's famous "Around-The-Island Swim" which would attract the world's top natators!

We could see a good movie for $1.25 evenings and 95¢ for a matinee! And they included such film fare as "The Snows Of Kilimanjaro", with Gregory Peck; "Springfield Rifle", starring Gary Cooper and "The Wild Heart", with Jennifer Jones. Singer-pianist Bob O'Neill was appearing at the Hialeah Club.

Evening classes at the Vocational Technical High School on Illinois Avenue and at the Junior High School were becoming increasingly popular. Courses included television repair, oil burner repair, welding, dramatics, and lampshade-making!

"Your Video Guide was published by Joseph Josephson Printers, 19 N. Virginia Avenue, Atlantic City between 1951 and 1956."

Atlantic City got its own commercial television station in December, the first factory-installed ultra high frequency station in the country! It was WFPG-TV, on UHF Channel 46. Hours of operation were 3 P.M. til midnight and it carried programs of the four major networks: NBC, ABC, CBS and Dumont!

Channel 46 continued operation until May of 1954, when it was decided to pull the plug due to lack of local advertising and problems of conversion of existing sets. But while it lasted, Channel 46 gave its viewers one beautiful picture!

Some of 1952's top tunes included "Detour", "The Roving Kind", "Please Mr. Sun" and "Tell Me Why". And did you know Atlantic City had its own string band then? It was so good, CBS Radio broadcast it coast-to-coast on Saturday afternoons! Horace Blitz was the announcer.

1953

It was only 47 years old, but was said to have lost its usefulness, so one of Atlantic City's most famous landmarks, Captain John L. Young's mansion on Million Dollar Pier felt the wrecker's ball in March. Captain Young had built the unusual structure in 1906 when he built the pier and over the years had filled it with a collection of rare pieces of furniture and statuary. It had been closed for a number years, but at one time was a top attraction in town.

So famous was Young's home out over the ocean that mail addressed merely to "#1 Atlantic Ocean" was delivered without delay! Presidents William Howard Taft and Theodore Roosevelt had been entertained there by Captain Young. In addition to the unusual furniture, Young fitted his mansion with rugs, chandeliers and objets d'art from all over the world. A museum had been planned there but the idea died aborning, in favor of more room for amusements on the big pier.

As we look back at the 50's from the vantage point of the 80's, we're grateful that the dread disease polio has been vanquished! But in 1953, local papers reported more cases than in 1952, which was an epidemic year, with more than 57,000 cases, 3,300 of which were fatal!

Atlantic City High School fielded its first undefeated and untied football team in 25 years! Jay Margerum was chosen first team all-state halfback and John Kelly was named as second team guard. Coach John Boyd led the Vikings in their undefeated season amid the tumultuous cheers of thousands of fans.

Our first motel, John's Motel opened that year, at Sovereign and Pacific Avenues, with eight units.

1953 saw a church "Skillo" game, in Newark, cited as gambling and there was local concern that the ruling might have a negative effect on the same game on our boardwalk! Albert A. Marks, Jr. was serving as president of the Community Chest, now The United Way, with John P. Milligan as Campaign Chairman. The goal that year was $174,212.

At a meeting of Atlantic City Commission, the final reading of the budget was adopted with no protests from those taxpayers present. The budget showed a tax rate of $13.26 per $100 of valuation. Director of Public Safety Thomas Wootton gave strict orders to police for a crackdown on sellers and carriers of switchblade knives.

Lady wrestlers were grunting and groaning at Convention Hall with a world title match, in March, between Mildred Burke and Mae Young. Ventnor marked its Golden Anniversary that year.

You'll probably be able to sing or at least hum, some of our popular songs of that year: "Somewhere Along The Way", "Wheel Of Fortune", "How Much Is That Doggie In The Window", "Til I Waltz Again With You", and "Your Cheatin' Heart".

1954

This was the one we'd been waiting for . . . our Centennial year, with many of those plans made three and four years earlier reaching fruition. On the first day of that bright new year, 50,000 visitors packed the city amid temperatures in the 50's!

A mammoth dinner party was held March 2nd, in Convention Hall, to mark our 100th birthday and everyone was invited! The cost: $5 per person. It was indeed a night to remember, with many of the town's early residents in attendance.

We were quite proud of our picturesque "Centennial Train" which made daily trips along the boardwalk carrying displays depicting the colorful story of Atlantic City during its first century. Two 50-foot tall promotional lighthouses were built on the White Horse and Black Horse Pikes and began flashing their bright beams in mid-January, calling attention to our Centennial year!

Scores of top-notch performers were seen here in 1954, forming a long and star-studded list! Dean Martin and Jerry Lewis appeared in person at the 500 Club, the spot where they had teamed up eight years before! Paul Whiteman was originating his show in the resort on ABC TV, and Larry Steele and his "Smart Affairs of 1955" held the spotlight at the Club Paradise on North Ohio Avenue.

Billy Kretchmer's jazz group was on stage at the Famous Club, Massachusetts and Pacific, and Jackie "Moms" Mabley was laughing it up at the Cotton Club, along with the dance team of "Stump and Stumpy".

A huge Mambo dance show was staged at Convention Hall on the 4th of July featuring the Gene Krupa Trio, the George Shearing Quintet, the Joe Loco Quintet, Candido, the Terry Gibbs Quartet and the Lee Konitz Quintet.

Perennial stripper Georgia Sothern was on stage at the Globe Burlesque on the 'Walk at Delaware Avenue, while the statesque (six feet-four) Lois De Fee was packin' 'em in at the Yacht Club.

Continuing with the list of big names playing the resort during our Centennial summer, Lanny Ross, Julius La Rosa, and the Mills Brothers were at Steel Pier in the Music Hall Theatre. Name bands, which appeared in the Marine Ballroom, included Spike Jones, Claude Thornhill, Hal McIntyre, Ralph Flanagan, and the Billy May Orchestra.

Of course, there was "Dancing Nightly Under the Stars" by the pool of the Brighton Hotel on the Boardwalk at Indiana Avenue. Ice Capades of '55 took over Convention Hall with such talented performers as Donna Atwood, Bobby Specht, Alan Conrad, and "The Old Smoothies".

The very first motel on our boardwalk opened in July, and was called, what else but . . . The Boardwalk Motel! It was located at Rhode Island Avenue.

The old Garrett house at Connecticut and Atlantic was demolished to make way for a new Acme Market. The old dwelling had been vacant and boarded up since about 1913. Now, the "new" Acme is gone too! Plans were being discussed for the restoration of Garden Pier, damaged by the hurricane a decade earlier. A total expenditure of $1,107,000 was envisioned.

New RCA television sets were selling for $159 to $795, depending on the model, and that was for black and white! If you were looking for a home in 1954, there was a good buy in Chelsea: a three-bedroom brick house, near the Richmond Avenue School for $8,750, and a Chelsea duplex was selling for $9,500! Firefighters Warren Conover, Kenneth Goff and Ed Jordan were promoted to Battalion Chiefs.

Local movie screens had such great epics as "The High And The Mighty", with Claire Trevor and John Wayne; "The Caine Mutiny", with Humphrey Bogart and Van Johnson, and "Magnificent Obsession", with Jane Wyman and Rock Hudson." When it came to songs, some of the year's new offering were "Three Coins in the Fountain", "Stranger in Paradise", "Little Things Mean a Lot", "Sh-Boom", and "I Left My Heart in San Francisco".

In the Atlantic City Press, nightclub proprietor Paul A. "Skinny" D'Amato was predicting that it would be our best year yet, and come to look at it, Skinny was right. It was a good one, from just about every point of view. Lots of visitors, good weather, a galaxy of top stars and a big increase in residential building which soared to 3.7 million dollars that year!

1955

What a hangover Atlantic City had after that year-long celebration marking its 100th birthday! But it quickly recovered after all the frivolity and fun and settled down to a normal "business-as-usual" pace, continuing to play host to millions of visitors. Surplus revenue in the county budget, at the end of 1954, was $300,000 plus, and the building boom on Absecon Island continued, so it appeared that another good year was in the offing.

Two new supermarkets opened on the Island that year: an Acme at the corner of Connecticut and Atlantic, and the Food Fair on Douglas Avenue, in Margate. Phone booths were erected along the boardwalk at street ends for the convenience of the public.

A town meeting was held, followed by formation of the Atlantic City Progress Council with George A. Hamid Jr., as Chairman. Arthur Broll was installed as president of the Greater Atlantic City Chamber of Commerce. Assemblyman Paul Salzberg became acting Governor of the state early in the year while Governor Robert Meyner vacationed in Florida.

An ice rink was proposed for Convention Hall Plaza, an idea that still refuses to die. The Federal Bureau of Narcotics was lauding our city for the fact that dope pushers and addicts were steering clear of our borders.

In sports, Nick Dirago, well-known coach and all-around sports star, was feted at a dinner in his honor at the 500 Club. And Rocky Castellani was making a bid for the middleweight boxing crown. A "Polar Bear" Club was active in the resort and members Luki Marcel, Joan Gordon, Louis Giannini, Joseph Rich, Sam Catanese, Dr. Joseph Carroll, Edward De Nick and Joseph Glasser devoted as much time as possible to physical fitness with an occasional dip in the surf, regardless of the temperatures, that winter! How cold was it? It was so cold that seals were spotted in Absecon Inlet by Louis Tomasello, a driver for the Brigantine Coach Company.

It was the inaugural season for our beautiful new Marina at Huron Avenue. Only two piers, of a projected total of 10, were operating, and they were busy all summer long. The second annual "Hotel and Restaurant Skills" Day was held in July under the guidance of Ada Taylor Sackett, originator of the event. City publicist, Mall Dodson, was the commentator describing the various categories, such as turkey carving, bedmaking, potato-paring, tray-carrying, and table-setting. It drew huge crowds each year it was held. Wonder why it was dropped?

Another "first" for '55 was the Atlantic City Marlin Tournament sponsored by the local Tuna Club. That first year, seven marlin were boated in two days of fishing.

The Reverend Richard Robinson, Pastor of First Baptist Church on Pacific Avenue, was bringing his message to large audiences via radio, with his popular "Joytime" broadcasts. In New York City, right on Broadway, a huge sign promoting our resort was erected, and a local contingent traveled to Manhattan to see it. They included Lou Cunningham, Bill Ruffu, Mike Fiore, John Sullivan, Gene Reardon, Ed Walsh, Adrian Phillips, Ezra Bell, Ed McNellis, Fred Chapman, Gay Langhorne, John Leachman, Henry Jamison and Charles Gross.

Entertainment-wise, things continued to jump, with such star performers as Jimmy Durante and his sidekick, Eddie Jackson, in person at the 500 Club; Arnett Cobb and Dakota Staton at Weekes' Lounge; Eddie Haywood and his "Rock and Roll Jazz Band" at the Paradise; Joan Weber, whose record of "Let Me Go, Lover" made her an overnight sensation, was appearing at Steel Pier, and in the Marine Ballroom that summer the walls echoed to the great music of Woody Herman and His Third Herd, Tony Pastor, Sauter-Finegan and Alex Bartha and their orchestras. And Johnny "Cry" Ray was sobbing on stage at the pier later in the season.

Further down the boardwalk at Million Dollar Pier, a dazzling aquatic display called "Dancing Waters" was a great crowd-pleaser! Ice cream soda freaks could really live it up with their favorite refreshment at the local Sun Ray Drug store for only 17¢! That was a "special", of course. The regular price was a quarter! The same store advertised salted Spanish peanuts at 43¢ a pound.

Margate City officials must have had great foresight because in 1955 that city purchased beach property between Argyle and Barclay Avenues for $7,500! And Mayor Eugene Tighe commented that the move put Margate in an excellent position to insitute beach fees! This was not to occur, however, until more than two decades later.

Voters were being urged to learn to use the new voting machines, and area civic clubs were displaying them at their meetings. Prior to that time, paper ballots were used.

Parking, then, as now, was a problem, and restaurateur Kenneth B. Walton was saying that the city had failed to plan in advance for the auto age. Walton pointed out that Atlantic City was founded as a "railroad town" and visitors were concentrated along Atlantic Avenue. But the auto, said Walton, changed all that with motorists trying to avoid that thorofare, and he suggested more off-street parking as a possible solution.

There was a movement afoot, begun by a local group, for a referendum to ban "live" music in licensed beverage establishments here on Saturdays, Sundays and holidays! So far as we can determine, the proposal never got off the ground.

Bids were being accepted for the installation of traffic lights on Atlantic Avenue, after the poles were removed, in the changeover from trolley cars to buses. Some 300 lights were to be put up between New Hampshire and Jackson Avenues.

AGE STEPS ASIDE FOR YOUTH
1865 - 1955
STREETCAR TO BUS
DECEMBER 28, 1955   ATLANTIC CITY, N.J.

Mervin E. Borgnis Collection

Max E. Blatt, veteran Atlantic City merchant, was planning to spend a million dollars to modernize his eight-story department store at South Carolina and Atlantic Avenues! He had opened the facility in 1922. It was later leased to Snellenberg's, then sold to Lit Brothers. It closed in 1977, due to lack of business, and at this writing is being converted to offices.

October was being observed as "Courtesy Month" in Atlantic City! Yes, even then courtesy was being touted as a most important prerequisite for our success, just as it is today! According to a published report, 40,000,000 meals were bought in Atlantic City by 13,000,000 vacationers that year! Willie Hartack and Sammy Boulmedies were the leading riders at the Atlantic City Race Course that season. And Jascha Heifetz, world renowned violinist, was signed to perform during that winter season for the local Community Concerts Association.

1956

Two decades before the successful casino referendum in Atlantic City, the subject was being discussed at great length among people "in the know" in the resort! It now appears they really were on to something! Paul "Skinny" D'Amato, owner of the 500 Club, came out in favor of it, stating it would do great things for the town. William Rich, proprietor of Ricky's Hialeah Club, was saying we'd have a boom town, with summertime business 52 weeks a year!

The Atlantic City Press had a column called "The Curious Cameraman" in those days, and on one occassion, six persons were asked how they felt about casinos here. They were equally divided pro and con.

Some officials of the Chalfonte-Haddon Hall opposed casinos here. It now seems quite ironic since that hotel became the very first casino to open for business, in 1978 as . . . Resorts International! Another hotel operation was quoted as being "cautiously in favor" of casinos, provided they were strictly supervised and regulated.

At a town meeting held by the progress committee in 1956, many suggestions were advanced including a Winter Jazz Festival, a broadened luxury tax, a college, a furniture mart, a library on Garden Pier and yes ... legalized gaming. So it would appear that even then the idea was there that someday, somehow, Atlantic City would have casinos!

Elsewhere on the local scene, Brigantine got natural gas. And residents were complaining about the U.S. Post Office hiking the price of mailing a letter from 3¢ to 4¢, and airmail from 6¢ to 7¢, and wondering where it would end! And gasoline! The cost of a gallon of fuel had soared from an average of 21.9¢ to as much as 25.9¢ for regular!

The Atlantic City Transportation Company leased a portion of Bader Field for a parking lot for automobiles. It cost a quarter to park up to 25 hours and one could take the bus to anywhere in Atlantic City or up Virginia Avenue to the Boardwalk for 15¢! At Chidsey-Chrysler-Plymouth, 3205 Arctic Avenue, one could buy a new Chrysler for $2,975, and a 4-door Plymouth Belvidere for $1,795.

Two local explorer scouts, John Voight and John Gottlieb, both aged 14, traveled to a scout pow-wow in Sweden! They were the only ones in the entire nation to make the trip and represented some 4,000,000 U. S. scouts!

The Around-The-Island Swim was again a big attraction and was won by Cliff Lumsden of Canada. Greta Anderson, of Denmark, and Tom Park, of California, finished second and third. A city ordinance now required taxicabs to have meters. Rates were to be 35¢ for the first ⅓ mile, 10¢ for each additional ⅓ mile and 20¢ for each additional passenger. Atlantic City hosted 330 conventions that year, up by seven from 1955.

Consolidation of the Downbeach communities with Atlantic City was a popular topic of discussion and Mayors Warren Titus of Margate and Eugene Tighe of Ventnor nixed the idea. Robert Leeds was installed as chairman of the boardwalk division of our Chamber of Commerce. Drive-in banking was the latest thing and folks were predicting it wouldn't be long before just about every bank would have it.

Singer Tony Bennett played Steel Pier that season, and so did the Mariners, the famous quartet featured on the Arthur Godfrey Radio Show for many years. The Pier emcee was the then-undiscovered comedian Frank Fontaine, who later became famous as "Crazy Guggenheim" on the Jackie Gleason Show! Buddy Morrow and His Orchestra played the Marine Ballroom and so did Woody Herman's Band. The singing rage, Miss Patti Page, played the 500 that summer and "The Drifters" appeared at Weekes' Lounge.

On local movie screens, 1956 was a year for some extra fine pictures: "Trapeze", with Burt Lancaster, "The Proud Ones", starring Robert Ryan, "The Searchers", with John Wayne, "The Eddy Duchin Story", starring Tyrone Power and Kim Novak, and "The Man With The Golden Arm", starring Frank Sinatra.

Evenings at home were spent watching such television fare as "Chance of a Lifetime", "The Millionaire", "Life Begins at 80", "Two for the Money", "Bishop Fulton Sheen", "Masquerade Party", and the news with John Facenda.

Governor Robert Meyner closed all our boardwalk games of chance by remote control from Trenton when he vetoed a bill which would have exempted them from the state's anti-gambling law. The year ended with many people still saying, "Let's open up some casinos here and get the old town back on the tracks!" They simply refused to let the idea die.

1957

This was another "very good year" for Atlantic City! Bank deposits for the Fourth of July weekend totalled more than $15,000,000, up some $4,000,000 over the previous year. City Commission okayed an expenditure of $46,500 for a master plan by a New York City firm to study traffic, parking, schools, population, recreation and the economy of the town. More than 150 private planes landed at Bader Field Easter weekend! Demolition work was completed on the old Earle Theatre, Missouri and Atlantic Avenues, which had been built in 1928.

Lincoln Transit took over the old Northside Trust bank building at Arkansas and Arctic Avenues, and converted it into a bus depot. Our police cars were equipped with two-way radios and flashing lights on the roof. 50,000 American Legionnaires marched on our boardwalk in a 10-hour parade that September. 10 lots on Absecon Boulevard were sold by Frank P. Gravatt at auction for only $118,000. Miss Maizie Scanlon was elected president of the New Jersey Education Association. The new Lombardy Motel opened in June, and free polio shots were being administered to more than 1,000 school students. Reverend Richard Robinson of First Baptist Church left to take a post with the Gospel Futherance Society.

Atlantic City's Dr. David B. Allman made national headlines when he was elected president of the American Medical Association, the first New Jerseyan to achieve that honor! Pete Schaeffer was installed as president of the Chamber of Commerce. Actress Tallulah Bankhead visited our town, then went to the local race course to play the ponies.

Alfred's Italian Restaurant on Maryland Avenue, just off the Boardwalk, was being enlarged following the purchase of Jack Carr's Theatrical Bar. Two hotels were destroyed by fire in March: the six-story Merion and the five-story Sunny Seas, both on Oriental Avenue. "Skinny" D'Amato was given the Press Club's award for doing the most to spread the name and fame of Atlantic City.

The Garwood Mills Discount Shopping Center opened in March in the old car barn buildings at Caspian and New Hampshire Avenues, the first store of its kind in this area. Mayor Altman was urging hotel, motel and rooming house owners to contribute 10 percent of their income, during the huge American Legion Convention, to the Legion's Convention Corporation as a gesture of gratitude and good faith.

Our $1,000,000 Atlantic City Marina was dedicated, in September, with 100 decorated vessels taking part in the ceremonies. Senator "Hap" Farley, for whom the Marina was later re-named, officiated, along with the Mayor. A.C.H.S. football coach John Boyd was saying athletes were the best-behaved students, due to their training in discipline.

Public Safety Director Thomas B. Wootton died at the age of 63, following a stroke, and Meredith "Todd" Kerstetter was sworn in to fill Wootton's unexpired term. Our 103 year old hand-drawn, hand-operated pumper was unveiled to the public, completely restored! The venerable piece of fire apparatus was put back into tip-top shape by the Atlantic City Association of Insurance Agents. It was the city's very first-pumper and is now on display in the Fire Museum of Atlantic County, located on Ryon Avenue, in Pleasantville.

Former Miss America Yolande Betbeze took a fling at show biz, appearing in "Bus Stop", on stage at the Chelsea Hotel's Playhouse that summer. After the season's receipts were toted up at City Hall, luxury taxes amounted to $803,521, ahead of 1956 by about $77,000.

On the entertainment scene such luminaries as Jerry Lewis, Carmen MacRae, Noro Morales, The Billy Williams Quartet, Frank Parker, The Four Lads, Les Elgart and His Orchestra, Dinah Washington, and Guy Mitchell all played Atlantic City that summer. Movie-goers enjoyed Fred Astaire and Cyd Charise in "Silk Stockings", Kim Novak and Jeff Chandler in "Jeanne Eagels", Cary Grant and Deborah Kerr in "An Affair To Remember", and "The Ten Commandments".

And do you remember these songs from 1957? "Don't Forbid Me", "Melodie D'Amour", "Seventy-Six Trombones", "My Special Angel", and "Bye Bye Love".

1958

A concerted effort to bring back legitimate theatre to our town was being made and the first show was "Drink To Me Only", which played the Warren Theatre on the Boardwalk near Arkansas Avenue. Actually, the Warren was merely the new name for the old Warner, with the letters rearranged. Michael Fiore was head of the theatre movement and there was much excitement and enthusiasm generated as people recalled the "glory days" of live theatre here in the 20's and 30's.

We had a record budget of $5,169,922 that year. The Ritz Carlton hotel was purchased by the Sheraton chain for a reported $4,250,000. Many residents of our city were not too happy to learn their drinking water supply had quietly been flouridated, after an earlier referendum had turned down the proposal. Richards' Baths, long a landmark on the wooden way was razed. In May, Our Lady of Lourdes Pageant was held with 150,000 people in attendance.

Local firefighters began working a 56-hour week. They had been putting in 70! The Weather Bureau left its Rhode Island Avenue headquarters and established a center in Pomona at the invitation of the Airways Modernization Board, which had taken over the old U. S. Naval Air Station there and created NAFEC, The National Aviation Facilities Experimental Center, now the Federal Aviation Administration Technical Center.

Suzanne Bruni, of the well-known hotel family, was Miss Atlantic City, and Mary Ann Mobley wore the crown of Miss America. Fire destroyed the home of former Senator Emerson Richards on the Boardwalk at South Carolina Avenue, including numerous art treasurers and a $100,000 organ.

The Italian community dedicated a handsome statue of Christopher Columbus on October 12, in what is now known as Columbus Plaza at Arkansas Avenue and Atlantic. Our beautiful fountain of light at Park Place and the Boardwalk was restored, and relighted. The Jewish Community Center opened in Margate. It had been located for many years on Virginia Avenue in Atlantic City. Atlantic City High School lost night football due to reported gang violence following a number of games.

100 war veterans were granted licenses to sell ice cream on the beach, and 18 women from our school patrol began special duties as boardwalk police officers. Samuel Meth was named "Hotel Greeter of the Year".

Red Buttons played Steel Pier that summer, and Johnny "Rubber Face" Frisco appeared at Nick Talley's. Singing star Buddy Greco and

His Quartet were in for the season at the Punch Bowl of the Brighton Hotel, which would be torn down later that year. It had opened in 1876.

At local movie houses, we could see "Kings Go Forth", with Frank Sinatra, "South Pacific", with an all-star cast headed by Mary Martin and Ezio Pinza, which played the Virginia Theatre for months, "King Creole", starring Elvis Presley, "No Time For Sergeants", with Andy Griffith and "Bridge on the River Kwai", which played the Beach Theatre on the Avenue for more than four months!

Some of the new songs we sang were: "Chanson D'Amour", "The Hawaiian Wedding Song", "Thank Heaven for Little Girls", "Volare" (Nel Blu, Depinto Di Blu) and the cute Christmas novelties "Rockin' Around the Christmas Tree", and "The Chipmunk Song".

Souvenir Post Card Co., N. Y.

1959

In April, "The Honeymooner", the daily Pennsylvania Reading Seashore Lines train, made her final run. It had been a regular out of Philadelphia for about 40 years. Michael Fiore headed the Chamber of Commerce for his second term and two popular Atlantic City policemen, John Sochocky and William Shepperson received the "Policeman of the Year" award from the Elks Club, for their outstanding work on behalf of our youth.

A tragic note was recorded when the Grace Lines' cruise ship Santa Rosa collided with an empty tanker off our coast and four of the tanker's crew died. The Senior Citizen Day Care Center opened in the Richmond Avenue School. An old Atlantic City landmark, the Elberon Hotel, at Tennessee and Pacific Avenues, was the victim of demolition to make way for modern construction, while the Royal Palms Hotel, on

Maryland Avenue, left the scene as the result of a fire.

Augustine A. Repetto, resort attorney, became the Atlantic County Prosecutor. Governor Robert B. Meyner and our Mayor, Joseph Altman, officially opened our huge China and Glass Show in January.

The new American flag now sported 49 stars as Alaska was admitted to the Union, but the city decided it would use up all of its old 48-star banners before buying new ones. Turf expert J. J. Williams had a local office for those seeking information from a horse racing consultant "with a good track record". One could purchase a beautiful new Studebaker "Lark" from Mathis Motor Company for $1,795, delivered!

Some of the songs popular that year include: "Deck of Cards", "High Hopes", "See You in September", "El Paso", and "My Favorite Things".

Attendance records were set when teen idol Ricky Nelson played Steel Pier, with his guitar, singing his current hits. And not only young people rushed to see Ricky! I recall mobs of adults on the ship's deck on the east side of the pier, waiting for a glimpse of the young star as he left by limousine after each show.

Childs' "Gay 90's" on the boardwalk packed 'em in with singing waiters, old time songs performed by costumed singers and lots of good, clean fun. Menasha Skulnik starred at the Warren Theatre in "The Law and Mr. Simon".

Frank Sinatra appeared at the 500 Club that August, along with jazz musician Red Norvo and Pete Miller and His Orchestra, the house band there for many seasons. Maybe you were among the hundreds standing in line to get in to see Frank!

Jackie Wilson sang at the grand opening of the new Coliseum, Baltic and Arkansas Avenues, where Sil Austin and His Orchestra shared the bill. Admission was only $2.

The King of Hi-de-Ho, Cab Calloway had star billing in the Submarine Room of the Traymore Hotel, and Joel Grey, Phil Foster, Fran Warren and Milton Berle kept us entertained that summer season as one after another came to the aforementioned 500!

Back at Steel Pier, crowds applauded such top attraction as Gene Krupa and His Orchestra, The Three Stooges, Frankie Avalon, Buddy Rich and His Band and The Four Lads.

The silver screen in '59 offered "The Diary of Anne Frank", "The Nun's Story", "The Horse Soldiers", "This Earth is Mine" and "Auntie Mame", starring the delightful Rosalind Russell.

1960

A commuter airline service was established at Bader Field by Seaboard Airlines, which advertised 20-minute flights between the resort and Philadelphia for $8, one way. Judge Leon Leonard was lamenting the fact that it was becoming increasingly difficult to secure jurors! Atlantic City employees received pay raises ranging from $120 to $300 per year.

The New Jersey Hotel Association joined the trend and re-named itself the Hotel-Motel Association at a meeting held at the Claridge and named Martin Shamberg as their new president. Our boardwalk was being re-decked for about 23 blocks at a cost of $700,000, while $3,500,000 was being spent on improvements to Convention Hall.

The city opened a second municipal parking lot on Illinois Avenue where the old Atlantic City lumber yard had stood. Gray's Restaurant, on the 'walk opposite Steel Pier, was leased to Arthur Maisel of New York and Miami Beach.

Mayor Altman was trying to hold the tax rate below the $10 mark. 1959's tax rate was $9.70. The colorful one-time Republican leader of the city and county, Enoch "Nucky" Johnson, marked his 77th birthday. The "welcome" booths of the Jaycees made their return on the Black Horse and White Horse Pikes leading into our city, inviting motorists to stop for information. Warren Cornelius was installed as president of the local NAACP and L. Edison Mathis was named to head the Greater Atlantic City Chamber of Commerce.

Steak was selling for 79¢ a pound, canned soup was one dollar for 11 cans! And we could mix-and-match any of the following for a buck: seven cans of corn, four cans of peaches, five cans of tuna, and five one-quart cans of apple juice!

The Volkswagen continued to gain popularity and we could buy the latest model at Specialty Motors on North Iowa Avenue for $1,565, fully equipped and delivered! A local student, Henry G. Broome, Jr., now an attorney and judge, attended the G-O-P Convention, in Chicago, and served as a Sergeant-At-Arms, one of only 14 students statewide to be chosen! A group of resort V.I.P.'s was entertained on board the palatial yacht "Potomac", tied up at the Inlet. The vessel had served former President Franklin D. Roosevelt. The "Potomac" was here for the summer, and her owners, Neptune Lines of Camden, offered luxury cruises up and down the coast.

In the wonderful world of entertainment, singer Vic Damone was at the 500 Club. Kathy Keegan sang at the Traymore and the calypso craze, then sweeping the nation, was being enjoyed here with "The Duke of Iron" appearing in the El Toro Room of the Madison Hotel. And that Frank Sinatra "look-alike, sound-alike", Duke Hazlett, was at Le Bistro. Later that season, the Real McCoy, old blue eyes himself, returned to his favorite local spot, the 500 Club for a 10-day engagement.

The Atlantic City Jazz Festival at the Coliseum featured a long list of top stars including Count Basie and His Orchestra, with Joe Williams, Sarah Vaughan, Julian "Cannonball" Adderly, Dave Brubeck, Art Blakey and His Jazz Messengers, Gerry Mulligan, Lambert, Hendricks and Ross, Dinah Washington, Oscar Peterson, Dakota Staton, Ray Charles and His Orchestra and Gloria Lynn. The one and only "Symphony Sid" was the emcee for the affair!

At the movies: "Happy Anniversary", starring David Niven, "Operation Petticoat", with Cary Grant, "The Wreck of the Mary Deare", featuring Gary Cooper, "The Gene Krupa Story", starring Sal Mineo, and "The Apartment", with Jack Lemmon.

And we had some really good songs that year: "Wonderland By

Night", "Hey, Look Me Over", "Put on a Happy Face", "The Second Time Around", and "If Ever I Should Leave You".

1961

A blizzard, in January put the city, in a deep freeze with temperatures of 15 degrees and winds up to 44 m.p.h.! Things were at a standstill until digging out operations began. Rail cuts on PRSL by the Public Utilities Commission were being strongly opposed by commuters who depended on those trains. The line had 3,000 daily riders at that time! Later in the season, they tried out excursion trains on Sundays between Atlantic City and Philadelphia, but the old spark was gone. Visitors preferred using their cars!

Dr. Hilton S. Read, founder of the famed Ventnor Foundation received the "Brotherhood Week" award. Dr. Read, also, was written up in Readers' Digest for his fine work. Leon Leonard was sworn in as a Superior Court Judge and Albert H. Skean, former head of our Convention Bureau, was appointed to the Convention Hall Advisory Board.

In sports, former Olympic rowing champion Jack Kelly was guest speaker at the All Sports Association's installation dinner. The late Senator "Hap" Farley was the Master of Ceremonies. The Atlantic City Marlin Club won the Tuna Tourney, with Bill Scott's 59-pounder setting a record!

The Around-The-Island Swim was won by Herman Willemse of Holland for the second consecutive year! He navigated the 25-mile course in 11 hours, 14 minutes, 45 seconds. Greta Anderson came in second with Cliff Lumsden third.

Atlantic City became one of 300 so-called "pilot" cities for a nationwide improved mail service experiment to speed up delivery. The annual "Powder Puff Derby", an all-woman air race from San Diego, California, again made Atlantic City its eastern terminus. Commissioner William F. Casey headed up the county Republican party. The Atlantic City Beach Patrol moved to its new quarters at 2318 Atlantic Avenue.

The popular "Gay 90's" night at the Betty Bacharach Home, then located in Longport, again proved to be a resounding success with many entertainers from area clubs donating their talents to help the institution. Those affairs were held out of doors and proved to be one of the highlights of the summer season.

And to prove there's nothing new, television violence was being assailed by many local people who said they were appalled and sickened by the number of murders, shootings, muggings and other mayhem depicted on home screens! They said something just had to be done about it!

Again, top entertainers played Atlantic City including Frances Faye at the 500 Club, Sonny Kendis and His Orchestra at the Ritz, The Pastors: Guy, Tony and Tony, Jr., at the Gondola Room, along with singer Dick Haymes. Pianist Hazel Scott shared billing with comedian Guy Marks at The Black Orchid.

Booked into Steel Pier that summer were: Paul Anka, Chubby Checker, George Gobel, and Dick Clark and His All-Star Show. In September, Hollywood screen star Joan Crawford was a Miss America Pageant judge.

At that time, our population stood at 59,544.

1962

March 6, 1962, has gone down in the record books of the Atlantic City weather station as a day that was almost unbelievable! An unusual combination of wind, tides and moon caused a situation that created havoc in every seashore community up and down the coast. Atlantic City was hard-hit, but so were many other cities and towns!

The storm had begun in a quiet way, when, in the morning, rain became mixed with large, fluffy flakes of snow! I usually drove to the studio from the mainland but something told me to use the bus that day! Enroute to Atlantic City, we could see waves from the bay already breaking over the Albany Avenue Boulevard! The wind had kicked up and it didn't look good. Ominous dark clouds hung overhead, and the bus passengers were noticeably concerned.

On Absecon Island, we're used to high tides, but this time, things would be different. Tides from the Atlantic Ocean and from the back bays met in the middle of the Island. Everything in the path of the water was at its mercy: homes, stores, automobiles, hotels. Yes, hotels because the water rose so quickly and to such a depth that there was little time to take steps to prevent it from entering the buildings.

The Morton Hotel on Virginia Avenue, used countless sandbags at the entrance but they did little good. The ocean had rolled under the boardwalk and up the avenue so that water stood at least three feet deep til the point where Virginia Avenue rises a bit, just below Pacific Avenue. Cars, which had been parked there earlier, became victims of the ravages of salt water. Once their engines and transmissions had become submerged, the damage was done.

Many residents lost everything except the clothes on their backs, or perhaps the few belongings they were able to salvage in their haste to escape the rising water. The Red Cross and Salvation Army were taxed to the fullest, working around the clock. Many say the March, 1962 storm was far worse than the 1944 hurricane!

Under ordinary circumstances, the water would have receded in a few hours, but as it was, it remained the following day, since it had nowhere to go. But it finally ran off and the massive cleanup job began, involving thousands of workers and thousands of hours.

The underpass between Virginia Avenue and Steel Pier was blocked by beach sand for a couple of weeks, and the pier was cut in half by a runaway barge which went right through it on its way to Ventnor! I was among some of the staff of WFPG marooned on the pier for two days, and we supplied news of the storm and other vital information until our transmitter became awash, and we went off the air!

March can be capricious, but in 1962, she went just a bit too far!

Anyone who lived through that harrowing experience will remember how it was, for a long time to come!

A master plan was presented that year, too. Total cost, spread over a 30-year period, was to be $29,000,000. It included a cultural center near the Inlet, sports and theatre center, an aquarium on Garden Pier, a Northside recreation center, playgrounds, two "par three' golf courses, street widening and new bridges. Murray Bisgaier, of the Community Housing and Planning Association, and Albert B. Johnson, chairman of the Planning Board, explained the plan to the public.

Chamber of Commerce Executive Director Al Owen was instrumental in convincing the local weather station to use the term "partly sunny" rather than "partly cloudy" in their forecasts, and it continues to this day. It was Owen's contention that if part of the day was to be cloudy, the other part must be sunny, so why not accentuate the positive!

George A. Hamid Sr. was honored by the Poor Richard Club of Philadelphia for his philanthropy. Boardwalk patrols were beefed up by Police Chief Jerry Sullivan. Local nightclubs were jumping that summer with such stars as Adam Wade at the Hialeah, Damita Jo at the Harlem, Enzo Stuarti at Luigi's, Della Reese at The Black Orchid. Bobby Vinton at the Hialeah later in the season, and Fran Warren and George Auld and His Orchestra at the 500 Club.

Popular songs included "Alley Cat", "Release Me", "Crying in the Rain", "A Little Bitty Tear", and "Ramblin' Rose".

1963

Urban renewal for Atlantic City was in the survey stage, under the guidance of Pauline Hill of the Housing Authority. The area being considered took in 88 acres between Connecticut and Virginia Avenues from Atlantic Avenue to the Boardwalk. Mrs. Hill called it "good buisness" suggesting that the tract would be the site of townhouses, shops, a theatre, and even a seaquarium. Just about every home situated within those boundaries was torn down, and as it lay idle for many years, it came to be known as "Pauline's Prairie". Right now, it is used to park thousands of vehicles , in huge parking lots. But there are big plans in the offing, including casinos.

Believe it or not, but the city had only two banks as recently as 1963: the Boardwalk National and the Guarantee Trust! Deposits in both institutions for the Fourth of July holiday came to $22,222,630, which is some indication of the amount of business transacted. The Atlantic City Expressway, which would become a major artery between Camden and Atlantic City, was only on the drawing boards then. A Convention Hall Annex was under discussion and is now an actuality as West Hall or Stetson Hall.

Philadelphia exotic dancer, Lillian Reis, was back in town after creating quite a stir by giving an exhibition of the then popular dance craze, "The Twist", at a New York Avenue club which had caused authorities to raise their eyebrows. She had been asked to leave town and had done so. But now she was back! And it seems she stayed awhile, and the furor died down.

People were complaining that the newly-instituted zip code of the U. S. Postal Service only gave them another number to remember. 80 planes were entered in the annual Powder Puff Derby with women pilots flying to the resort from California.

On Friday, November 22, Atlantic City and the nation were plunged into shock by the news that President John F. Kennedy had been assassinated in Dallas, Texas! Meetings were cancelled, students were sent home from school, stores closed and a pall fell over all regular activity! As in the case of Pearl Harbor, those who remember that day can recall where they were and what they were doing when they learned of the President's death.

For the first time in its long history, the Morris Guards honored a female for heroism. She was 12-year-old Dale Peterson who had rescued a woman from a burning building. Jay Trilling was selling paint in his Atlantic Avenue store for $3.96 a gallon and singing its praises over the radio to the tune of "Put On Your Old Grey Bonnet".

Steel Pier again played host to hundreds of thousands that summer as it featured more than 40 top names including Chubby Checker, Ed McMahon, Bobby Darin, Donald O'Connor, and the orchestras of Stan Kenton, Si Zentner, Les Elgart, Johnny Austin and Ralph Marterie.

Louis Tussaud's Wax Museum opened on the boardwalk with a number of famous persons on display, people bearing remarkable likenesses to their real life counterparts, complete to authentic costumes. Beach Patrol Chief Richard Hughes said that 160,000 persons were on the sands for the season opener in July. A gigantic fireworks display on the "fourth" was praised by our merchants as a real shot in the arm for business.

You could buy a four-bedroom home, with ground floor apartment for $9,900! Operators of parking lots were complaining to authorities about a city ordinance forbidding them to openly solicit customers by waving them in. Edgar A. Harris, who later would become president of the Atlantic City N.A.A.C.P. won a National Science Foundation Scholarship for advanced study in mathematics.

Even then, there was talk of a high-speed route to the shore via a levicar system between here and Kirkwood, with the trip taking only 20 minutes! Renowned resort athlete, Joe Hackney, received a 50-year service pin from the American Red Cross and he's still going strong!

The cost of operating our public schools for the 1962-63 school year was $3,385,930, which was $8,601 over the budget. On the entertainment scene there was much to do and see! The 500 Club featured songstress Helen Forrest, a former Atlantic City gal, who went on to fame and fortune singing with not one, but three of the nation's name bands: Benny Goodman, Harry James and Artie Shaw! Miss Forrest shared the bill that summer with another localite, trumpet star Ziggy Elman who as a teenager, had joined Goodman's band at Steel Pier while playing with Alex Bartha's Orchestra.

Sam Cooke was at the Harlem, Jack Jones at Le Bistro, Lloyd Price at the Hialeah, Jimmy McGriff at the Wonder Gardens, Tommy Edwards and Thelma Carpenter at Basin Street and Wild Bill Davis at Grace's Little Belmont!

Other name stars appearing in town that year were Bob Eberly, Lionel Hampton, Brenda Lee, Lou Monte, Vaughn Meader, Bobby Vinton, Dick Clark, and Bobby Rydell.

At the movies we saw "Bye Bye Birdie", "Come Blow Your Horn", "55 Days at Peking", "Spencer's Mountain", and "Lawrence of Arabia". And some fine TV shows kept us at home: "Wagon Train", "Dobie Gillis", "Naked City", and "The Johnny Carson Show". And 1963 gave us songs like "Blame It On The Bossa Nova", "My Coloring Book", "Call Me Irresponsible", "Painted, Tainted Rose", and "Washington Square".

And while life went on as usual during another typical Atlantic City summer, plans were being made to welcome a really large delegation the following year. The Democratic National Committee had chosen our town as the site for its national convention!

1964

Where would we park all the cars and where we would house all the people who would converge on our city during the Democratic National Convention? That was the $64,000 question! It all worked out somehow and proved to be the high spot of the summer . . . the week we rolled out the red carpet for that conclave! Lyndon Baynes Johnson was nominated as the party's standard-bearer and we had fireworks every night during the convention!

The Atlantic City Expressway opened on July 31, and carried 50,000 vehicles on its first weekend in business. A building with three apartments on Bellevue Avenue could be bought in 1964 for $9,500. Special buses were running from the city to the New York World's Fair and the cost was only $7.75 round trip! Luxury tax collections were off by more than $17,000 for July. Our Convention Hall got a new lighting system at a cost of $100,000, and the beautiful old Dennis Hotel marked its 100th birthday that year!

Construction began on the Brighton Towers apartment complex on Atlantic Avenue. Tuition at the high school increased to $431.40 per student, per year. A new record was set during the Marlin Tourney that summer with a 620-pound Blue Marlin boated after a hard fight!

At local markets, ground beef was selling for 43¢ a pound; bacon, 49¢ a pound; boiled ham, 78¢ a pound; flounder, 39¢ a pound and celery, 19¢ a stalk. And we received green stamps, too! In September, the Grand Marshal for the Miss America Pageant parade "was the hostess with the mostest", Pearl Mesta. The Plaza in front of Convention Hall was dedicated that August by Governor Richard Hughes, as John F. Kennedy Plaza and a bust of the late President, sculpted by EvAngelos Frudakis of Philadelphia and Ventnor. The bust was commissioned by a Republican, Senator Frank S. "Hap" Farley! The Beatles appeared, in person, in Convention Hall!

Local night clubs sparkled with top stars such as Jackie Mason and Myron Cohen at The Black Orchid, Ahmad Jamal at the Wonder Gardens, Gloria Lynn at Le Bistro, Johnny Nash at the Harlem and Joey Stevens at the 500 Club. Steel Pier, that summer of '64, had its share of names too: The Dukes of Dixieland, Russ Carlyle and His Orchestra, Milton Berle, and a quartet of stars from the Lawrence Welk TV Show: Jo Ann Castle, Myron Floren, and dancers Barbara Boylan and Bobby Burgess.

At the movies, we enjoyed such offerings as "The Long Ships", "Mad, Mad, Mad, Mad World", "The Unsinkable Molly Brown", "TheCarpetbaggers", and "Cleopatra".

Dixie Blandy, the well-known flagpole sitter, had completed 77 days in September, and crowds gathered daily and nightly to watch him perched high in the sky atop a pole on Steel Pier. He died some years later in a fall from a pole in a shopping center.

10292 HOTEL DENNIS, ATLANTIC CITY, N. J.

1965

This was another good one for Atlantic City, and during the summer months, tourists by the thousands came to see such top entertainers as Louis Armstrong, Gary Lewis and The Playboys, Brenda Lee, Frank Fontaine, George Gobel, The King Family, Wayne Newton, Herman's Hermits, Johnny Mathis, Peter and Gordon, and Larry Hooper of the Lawrence Welk Show, all of whom played Steel Pier the summer of '65.

A good meal could be had at Arthur Maisel's Restaurant, opposite Steel Pier, for only 99¢ including free coffee. Efforts were being made to attract foreign firms to our city. The Traymore Corporation filed bankruptcy papers, with the operation of the famous old hostelry being resumed by Lawrence and Preston Tisch. Debts were to be settled at 50¢ on the dollar.

Mayor Altman and impresario George A. Hamid Jr., concurred

that this would be our best season yet! A construction boom was underway and things were looking rosy, for the entire area, with a forecast that $900,000,000 would be spent in Atlantic City! Our hospital dedicated its new $189,000 cobalt unit for the treatment of cancer patients.

The Two Guys department store on Albany Boulevard opened in August. And the 8th of that month was recorded as the busiest day on the new Atlantic City Expressway since it was opened in 1964. More than 75,000 vehicles passed the Egg Harbor Toll Plaza with 40,000 of them continuing to Atlantic City! Atlantic Avenue merchants were taken to task by Director of Public Works, William F. Casey, for allegedly sweeping trash and refuse off their sidewalks into the gutters.

Our first "Little Miss Atlantic City", 10-year old Patricia Eileen Murphy, was crowned at the Quarterdeck Theatre of the Morton Hotel on Virginia Avenue. Luxury homes in the $25,000 to $75,000 price range were planned for a 75-acre section of Bayview Island, near Two Guys. The "Westy Hogan" trap shoot was attracting crowds to the range of Absecon Boulevard.

Two opera stars come to entertain us that summer. Baritone William Walker appeared at the Ventnor Summer Music Festival, and Tenor Richard Tucker was at the Hebrew Academy. Pioneer hotelman Ezra Bell died at the age of 73. He had been president of our Convention Bureau for 37 years and was well known in local hotel circles.

Police Chief Jerry Sullivan objected to members of the force subjecting themselves to a dunking at a "Gas Days For Charity" event at Cole's Corner Service Station, saying it was demeaning, but the Jaycees volunteered to fill the breach, and the show went on!

Recruiting for faculty at Atlantic Community College began for its temporary facility on the boardwalk in the Mayflower Hotel. And the "Elbo A-Go-Go" was advertising itself as "The Area's First Discotheque", a new word which was to take its place in our language very quickly.

1966

Reflecting 1965 business, Atlantic City's luxury tax receipts this year put the total over the $2,000,000 mark for the first time! The official tally was $2,000,990, the largest amount ever collected in the 19-year history of the tax. A spectacular $250,000 fire destroyed the Calvi Electric Company on Arctic Avenue, that January. Jack Karp was installed as president of the Greater Atlantic City Chamber of Commerce for his second term.

Rabbi Harry Jolt was calling for unity among Jewish congregations following his election as president of the Atlantic County Board of Rabbis. The Women's Basketball Association of America held an international tournament in Convention Hall. Two surfboard contests were announced by our tall, cigar-smoking city publicist, Mall Dodson. More than 200,000 persons were expected in town for the Independence Day holiday so Mayor Altman refused to issue a permit for the local Democratic Club to parade. The Mayor figured the city would have a bad time as it was, with heavy traffic. And speaking of traffic, the Atlantic City Parking Association was saying it saw no need for a Parking Authority.

The Rolling Stones, a rock group, appeared that summer on Steel Pier. Dionne Warwick drew thousands to the old showplace, as did another group called "The Cyrkle". Among the attractions in the Marine Ballroom were the Dukes of Dixieland, Bob Crosby and His Orchestra, and the Billy May Band, directed by Frankie Lester, a fine singer who sounded a bit like another Frank! Lester later would lead the Steel Pier "Big Band" which was featured for two seasons there. The old Globe Burlesque Theatre, Boardwalk at Delaware Avenue, opened for its 34th season. On other local stages, James Brown appeared at Convention Hall, Cab Calloway was starring at the Club Harlem, Jack E. Leonard at Le Bistro, and stripper Blaze Starr was at the Capitol on Atlantic Avenue.

Movies we enjoyed were "Born Free", "Doctor Zhivago", "Harper", "Assault On A Queen", and "The Oscar". When it came to songs, 1966 could boast some really good ones such as "Daydream", "Sunny", "That's Life", "Flowers On The Wall", and "Strangers In The Night".

The city's budget was $15,172,500 upping the tax rate by 46¢! The new Howard Johnson's Motor Lodge on Arkansas Avenue at Pacific, opened in July with Howard B. Johnson, president of the chain, on hand for the ceremonies. It cost $3,700,000. The temperature set a new record on July 4th when the mercury hit 99! We had an ice shortage due to the oppressive heat, and only one supplier, the Philadelphia-based American Ice Company! What a howl went up from restaurants, night clubs, boardwalk juice stands and bars! How could they operate without ice?

The city borrowed $1,930,000 from the Boardwalk National Bank on bond anticipation notes for the uptown urban renewal project. The bank charged 3.40% interest! The Madison Hotel on South Illinois Avenue was sold for $650,000. It later became a rest home operated by the Presbyterian Church.

Philip Wechsler was appointed Associated Press correspondent for Atlantic City. Phil now holds down the job of Public Relations Chief for Resorts International.

1967

This was the year Mayor Joseph Altman retired from office after 22 years of guiding the destinies of Atlantic City from the old City Hall at the corner of Tennessee and Atlantic Avenues. Many's the time I trudged up those worn wooden stairs with a heavy tape recorder to tape his weekly broadcast "The Mayor's Report to the People", aired Friday nights on WFPG. His driver, the late William "Whitey" Thomas, picked me up at the studio in a big white Buick convertible with the city seal emblazoned on its doors! It was quite an impressive car and many a visitor had been heard to comment favorably on it saying the vehicle had a certain aura about it which made it look like it "belonged" to Atlantic City!

When the Mayor retired, he was 75 years of age and in poor health. To fill his unexpired term, Director of Parks and Public Property Richard Jackson was named by his colleagues on the City Commission to be Mayor. Elsewhere on the political scene, Atlantic County Senator Frank S. "Hap" Farley was re-elected, with the G-O-P again winning big in the city and the county. Arthur Ponzio was appointed to fill the seat of the late Commissioner John A. O'Donnell as Director of Revenue and Finance.

A $130,000,000 urban renewal housing project was in the works for the uptown section of our city for one half of the total area which had been leveled for that purpose. Plans called for 200 townhouses, 800 middle income units, 500 luxury units, a 20-story motel and a 70-thousand square foot shopping mall!

The federal government halted the proposed expansion of the Post Office at Illinois and Pacific Avenues when city officials and others interested in maintaining property values in that area voiced strong opposition.

Pressure was being brought to bear by local black groups for a black City Commissioner. Carlos La Sane became the city's first such Commissioner in 1968 when he was named head to the Department of Parks and Public Property.

A student peace corps was organized at Atlantic City High School and at the same seat of learning, a state trooper, posing as a student, was instrumental in bringing about 36 arrests at the school on a number of charges.

Songs heard for the first time that year were "There's A Kind Of Hush" (All Over the World), "Ode To Billy Joe", "It Must Be Him", "Look of Love", and "My Cup Runneth Over".

1968

Premium giveaways were at their peak and gasoline stations were offering all manner of promotional items such as coins, toys, glassware, pictures, and those ever popular trading stamps! An assembly bill, aimed at halting the practice, was on the floor in Trenton and area service stations planned a one-day shutdown as a protest.

The annual Children's Boardwalk Parade was held in July with Ralph Taylor, its founder, as chairman. I recall driving my antique car in that parade carrying some delightful little cherubs who are now in high school! Atlantic City initiated a series of "Street Rock" programs designed to provide entertainment for the public on an informal basis, free of charge. The sites were changed each week with talent from area clubs performing.

One could buy a modern two-bedroom home and a store in Chelsea for $15,900! A shaggy, brown mongrel named "Duke", who was the official greeter at the State Marina for years, died of injuries suffered when he was hit by a car. The dog had been dropped off by a boat passing through 14 years earlier.

A trip to New York City via Public Service bus cost you only $7.20 ... round trip! In sports, boxer Emile Griffith was training in the area and basketball fans were thrilled at being able to watch the Philadelphia 76'ers and the Detroit Pistons at Convention Hall. Al Soifer was promoting wrestling there, with some of the matches featuring women.

Senator Frank Farley was being credited with swinging the New Jersey delegation over to Richard Nixon for President at the Republican National Convention, at Miami Beach. "Hap" was introduced on nation-wide television as "The Boss of the Boardwalk!"

The Reverend John J. McMenamin left St. Nicholas Church where he had been Pastor since 1955. Project "WILL", the only federally funded school program of its kind in the nation, was okayed for Atlantic City and N.A.A.C.P. President Edgar Harris was named to head it up. The urban renewal project, taking in the five-block area covering Virginia, Maryland, States, Delaware and New Jersey Avenues, ground to a halt when certain deals failed to materialize.

On the entertainment scene, the resort was not without its major attractions to lure visitors for a day, a weekend or a long vacation! The Steel Pier again featured a lineup filled with top names including the Cowsills, Pal and The Prophets, The Fifth Dimension, The Beach Boys, The Box Tops, and The New Christy Minstrels. Art Mooney and His Orchestra and The Jimmy Dorsey Band, directed by Lee Castle, also played the pier that summer. Theodore Bikel appeared, in person, in the Pennsylvania Room of Haddon Hall, presented by the Community Synagogue.

Teddy Lee and The Midnight Suns were featured in the Submarine Room of the Traymore, even then struggling to survive against massive odds as a result of the success of dazzling new motels, which were spring-ing up like mushrooms after a summer shower. Billy Daniels played the Club Harlem and Guy Marks starred at The Black Orchid.

Visitors to our town enjoyed the offerings of the Smithville Music Fair on the mainland, which had signed up some stellar attractions such as Victor Borge, The Doors, Joey Heatherton in "Can Can", and Ann Corio in "This Was Burlesque". At the movies we sat enthralled as we watched "The Detective" starring Frank Sinatra, "Rosemary's Baby", with Mia Farrow, plus "The Graduate", "The Green Berets", and "Where Were You When the Lights Went Out?".

1969

The Ten-Hundred block of Atlantic Avenue got a face-lift when the germ of an idea hatched in the mind of merchant Murray Raphel. Approx-imately half-a-million dollars were spent on the land and its preparation for a new approach to merchandising, which became the first pedestrian mall in the state: Gordon's Alley!

A modern high-rise apartment complex for senior citizens opened at New Hampshire and Melrose Avenues . . . the 14-story Inlet Towers. The resort's model cities program got a boost from a $154,000 grant. The Atlantic City Surfing Contest was held off the States Avenue beach, in June. The Atlantic City Transportation Company bus drivers went on strike July 1st, and 10,000 daily commuters had to find alternate means of getting to work.

The Special Investigation Squad of the Atlantic City Police Depart-ment made a record 85 arrests in June, according to Chief Mario Floriani, who would later become Atlantic County Sheriff. The city's third municipal parking lot opened on south New York Avenue, and another carefree throng of visitors poured onto our beaches and boardwalk, some 400,000 of them, that Fourth of July holiday!

An animal shelter was constructed on Absecon Boulevard by the County Humane Society. Harness racing under the lights was attracting thousands to the Atlantic City Raceway where man, animal and machine teamed up and left the gate following Bob Weems' thrilling cry of "There They Go-o-o-o-o!".

A ship caught fire at the city docks resulting in damage estimated at $300,000. She was the 297-foot research vessel "Atlantic Seal". Families, disrupted by the war in Viet Nam, were being reunited as veterans began returning home.

Terry Granger, a bright, young singing star, appeared at the Club Harlem with Larry Steele's "Smart Affairs of 1970". In the Submarine Room of the Traymore, we danced and romanced to the music of Ray Bloch and His Orchestra, and laughed at the comedy of Rossi and White. Damita Jo was at Le Bistro, where one could enjoy the show plus a good dinner for $5.95!

Steel Pier, that summer of 1969, featured Sandler and Young, Brooklyn Bridge, Leslie Gore and Mike Pedicin, but before year's end, tragedy would strike the big amusement center in the form of a disastrous fire, which destroyed the beautiful Marine Ballroom, the Ocean Stadium, home of the High-Diving Horse, and other parts of the big pier!

It happened on the evening of December 27, shortly after 6 P.M. I was notified, by phone, by one of our staff announcers, Dan Bradley, and immediately drove over! As I watched the old ballroom go up in smoke and flame, a lot of memories returned as I recalled many of the famous bands that had played that room where, for two decades, I had announced for scores of them on the air over CBS and ABC, between 1947 and 1967.

Over the years, millions of music fans had made the Marine Ballroom one of the most popular dance emporiums in the east! In a matter of a couple of hours, it was gone, never to be rebuilt. It was replaced after a fashion, by a modern structure called "The Golden Dome" and I saw the great Duke Ellington and His Orchestra there, but even he didn't sound as good as when he played the Marine Ballroom, with its great acoustics and huge dance floor. An era ended that winter's night and the ballroom's manager, Pat Cohen, and I have often reminisced about those great days when a different band would come in every week, all summer long.

And I'd be less than truthful if I said I didn't shed a tear or two for the sad death of the Marine Ballroom, in 1969. The pier was purchased by Resorts International in 1978, and no definite plans for its future have been announced. But the diving horses, "Dimah", "Gamal", and the others, dive no more, and the sounds of the big bands, whose members looked forward to being booked into the pier, are stilled. Someday . . . maybe . . . Steel Pier will and again claim the fame it enjoyed for 80 years!

The first March of Dimes Telethon was held at Manny Solomon's

Strand Motel and collected $11,455! Not bad for a start. In 1980, total collections amounted to $201,003!

1970

This was the year the Miss America Pageant parade on the Boardwalk returned to a night-time format. It had been an afternoon event for quite a few years, but due to public demand, Pageant officials decided to go back to the nocturnal presentation. And it has remained a night-time spectacle ever since. Lighting effects do much to enhance the beauty of the parade and the cool of evening makes it more pleasant to watch.

Charter buses entering Atlantic City paid an $18 fee to park and that amounted to $43,000 in 1970! The new police emergency telephone number 911 went into operation.

Local lifeguard and author, Joel Fogel, traveled via kayak from New York to Miami, studying the effects of pollution in the waters. Boxer Cassius Clay appeared at the opening of a local club that August. 18-year-olds got the vote in New Jersey. At A.C.H.S., students were issued I.D. cards. The city, even then, was mulling the idea of a beach fee, which at this writing still has not materialized, although just about every municipality along the Jersey coast has one. Another subject under discussion at that time was consolidation of all schools on Absecon Island and Brigantine.

Atlantic County Senator Frank S "Hap" Farley sought emergency funds of $600,000 to replenish our beaches, which had suffered much erosion during that year's winter storms. South Jersey Gas Company was planning a move from Atlantic City inland to Folsom, due to lack of space to expand their facilities.

The second annual March of Dimes Telethon netted a grand total of $47,669 for 54 hours on the air . . . a new record! Since that time, the figure has grown by leaps and bounds, with the same guiding force, radio personality Seymour "Pinky" Kravitz, putting it all together each February. Kravitz also organized our now famous Bal Masque that year!

A legislator from northern New Jersey, Union County Senator Frank X. McDermott, came up with a proposal to legalize casino gambling here and Senator Farley said he had no objections! Atlantic City Mayor William Somers said he favored gambling, so long as it was strictly supervised. That was the year Atlantic Prosecutor Robert McAllister admitted that the Mafia had made minor inroads into Atlantic City, but only in "small gambling operations, not like in the large cities".

In sports, Stan Bergman and Charles Wagner retained the Ventnor Beach Patrol rowing crown. Tuition at Atlantic City High School was hiked by $147 to $875.89 per year. A new daily newspaper was being considered for Atlantic City, but failed to go to press. On the world of entertainment, the summer of 1970 saw a parade of talent moving across the stages of cabarets, supper clubs and piers! The famous singing group, The Vagabonds, appeared at the 500, sharing the bill with impressionist Babe Pier, who later would star on Steel Pier in the ill-fated production of "Magic! Magic!", in 1978. Singing star Joe Valino was featured at Reds

Morgan's.

At George Hamid's Steel Pier, some of the big names that flashed from the marquee were Woody Herman and His Orchestra, Shelley Berman, Oliver, The Ides of March, London Lee, The Golddiggers, Frankie Valli and the Four Seasons, The Doodletown Pipers, and Chicago.

At the movies, we enjoyed such pictures as "A Man Called Horse", "Airport", "Darling Lili", "Rider On The Rain", and "Hello Dolly". Hit songs included "Everybody's Out of Town", "Where Do I Begin", "Sweet Caroline", "Winter World of Love" and "One Less Bell to Answer".

On July 20, "Lucy" the elephant was moved to her new home at Decatur Avenue and the Beach, from the spot at Cedar Grove Avenue, where she had stood staring at the ever-changing sea since 1881. It was quite an operation, requiring the cooperation of the utility companies, which had to move wires and other obstructions so that the huge pachyderm could lumber down the avenue with no problems.

Among the thousands witnessing the unusual event was 84-year-old John Lennig, who had at one time owned much of what is now the City of Margate. Lennig recounted how, as a boy of five, he had watched people dancing to the music of a piano located in the stomach of the elephant. Estimates of the cost of restoring the famous tourist attraction were set at $115,000, with the money to be raised by public subscription. At this writing, Lucy continues to thrill thousands each year, who go to see if she's really as big as she appears to be on those post cards. And she is!

1971

A show business legend and one of Atlantic City's staunchest supporters passed away, in 1971. He was George A. Hamid Sr., owner and operator of Steel Pier between 1945 and the time of his death. A dynamic man, Hamid rose to national prominence in his field. He had come to this country as a Lebanese acrobat, tumbling for coins on the beaches here in Atlantic City! He and I became good friends and I often marvelled at his expertise as he sat behind a microphone at WFPG, reeling off the highlights of what was taking place on the pier, in what he called his "little talks", before and after the Phillies games, year after year.

Douglas Fairbanks, Jr., visited our town and drew the names of winners in a contest conducted by a local drug store, in which he was a partner. I covered his arrival for WFPG and recall hordes of autograph seekers, especially women, descending upon that store!

Our state senators were split as to whether a bill for legalized gambling in Atlantic City would be approved by the legislature, in 1972. The cast of "No, No Nanette" were guests of the city, recalling the days when the famed Ziegfeld Follies played the boardwalk. The Barco Corporation failed to take title to four blocks in the city's urban renewal tract, causing further delay in the development of that part of town. The Atlantic City Boy's Club took over the old "Press" building at Virginia and Mediterranean Avenues, which had been given to them by the newspaper.

500 blue collar workers voted to join the AFL-CIO. Two new hous-

ing complexes, Shore Park and Shore Terrace, costing $11,000,000 to build, were dedicated on the city's northside. The taxpayer's organization "T.E.A.R.S." was trying to raise $50,000 to find a solution to cutting the city and county budgets. A single towing company was to be hired to replace the four then being used, to remove illegally parked vehicles.

8,000 Elks paraded on the 'walk that June. Public Safety Commissioner Mario Floriani announced free volunteer ambulance service in the city. Irving Ginsberg was installed as president of the Atlantic City Retail Merchants Association.

WFPG Radio personality, John Struckell, known to his legion of fans as "Captain John", died in August. John, who also was the station's general manager, had built a loyal and dedicated audience with his popular night-time program, "Music By The Sea", a combination of lush sounds and beautiful poetry.

Steel Pier played host to a dazzling lineup of top stars including Guy and Ralna of the Lawrence Welk Show, Chuck Berry, The Duprees, The Dovells, and Cab Calloway. At the movies, we could enjoy "The Summer of '42", at the Virginia, "Klute", at the Roxy, "The Anderson Tapes", at the Beach, "The Stewardesses", at the Strand and "Willard", at the Center.

And another batch of songs made their debut including "I'd Like To Teach The World To Sing", "The Look Of Love", "Old Fashioned Love Song", "Take Me Home, Country Roads", and "It's Impossible".

The 1970 census showed Atlantic City with a population of 47,859.

1972

Tropical storm "Agnes" hit the Atlantic seaboard that summer, leaving in its wake damage in the hundreds of thousands of dollars! But Atlantic City was spared the real impact of the storm and suffered only minor beach erosion, toppled signs and uprooted trees.

Senator George McGovern attended the convention of the National Education Association of 12,000 persons here. Another large gathering was that of the Elks, some 15,000 in number. They have met from time to time over the years in our resort, having come for the first time in 1894!

Atlantic City lost another of its loyal supporters when Charlie Seel, editor and publisher of the Atlantic City Reporter passed away while vacationing in Puerto Rico. Charlie, for many years, had a Sunday evening radio news program on WFPG and I was his announcer, starting in 1948.

Holy Spirit High coach Stan Marczyk was hired by the city to crack down on "jam joints" in the role of Boardwalk Inspector. And that was the year Jim Latz jogged 26 miles, long before it became the "in" thing. The Boy Scouts put on a colorful exhibition of historic flags on Garden Pier.

Commissioner Arthur Ponzio announced the planned demolition of a large section of the Inlet as part of urban renewal. In the entertainment world, Atlantic City saw some of the best talent available: Melba Moore at the Club Harlem, Lou Monte at The Black Orchid, and Steel Pier had Ray Eberle and The Modernaires, Peter Duchin and His Orchestra, and

The famous Hotel Traymore, on the Boardwalk at Illinois Avenue.

Jay and The Techniques.

At the Million Dollar Pier, people came to see the actual automobiles used in the film "The Godfather". And a man arrived in the area saying he wanted to "save" Lucy, the elephant, promising to donate $61,000 to the cause. He turned out to be an imposter.

We witnessed the destruction of our beautiful "Castle by the Sea", the Traymore Hotel, in a series of two planned implosions . . . demolition by charges set off so as to cause a building to fall into its own basement. The first took place in April, the second in May, and hundreds of onlookers swallowed hard as they watched the famous landmark at Illinois Avenue and the Boardwalk crumble, without a struggle, into a huge pile of rubble to make way for future development. The Traymore had been started as a small wooden structure in 1906, and was the center of conflict on a number of occasions as different groups fought to preserve the old hotel, while others were saying "let 'er go". Finally, it was decided to raze the Traymore rather than spend millions on repairs.

Atlantic City's "Merchant to the Rich" Reese Palley, chartered two 747 jets to carry 700 of his friends and customers to Paris, France to help him celebrate his birthday! Total bill came to roughly $250,000.

1973

Again, there was talk of trying to get the casino issue on the ballot for New Jersey, and both political parties backed the idea, at least in the polls taken around the state. However, at the voting polls the following year, it would be a different story, with the measure going down to defeat. But in 1973, lots of local people remained enthusiastic and really thought gambling state-wide had a chance . . . if not now, then someday.

Atlantic City hired Gerard Kauper, of the New York City Convention Bureau, to replace the late Wayne Stetson as Vice-President and General Manager of our Convention Bureau. In Stetson's honor, West Hall was re-named "Stetson Hall".

Jam joints continued to plague Boardwalk strollers, with the city promising to clamp down hard on their operations. The newly resurfaced tennis courts were opened at Bader Field. On the Fourth of July, square dances at Park Place proved to be a big drawing card, with hundreds watching the brightly-costumed dancers do-se-do-ing all over the place! Our big boardwalk "Bike-In" attracted some 2,000 cycling enthusiasts to the wooden way. And the trams first appeared on our boardwalk, causing many an old-timer to wonder what was happening!

Thomas O'Neill was seated as president of the Rotary Club, and the Atlantic City Merchants Association announced a discount of 10 percent for senior citizens. Some 33 firms voted to participate.

Localites were suggesting many innovative ideas to lure the visitors: dune buggy rides on the beaches, shell festivals, jogging contests and walkathons, "bloodless" bull fights at Convention Hall, and the ever-popular Aquarium!

Although things weren't as good as they used to be, we still got some name stars that summer. We enjoyed the songs of Don Cornell at Steel Pier, along with the famous "Big Band" directed by Frankie Lester. That was the "house" band then, which was featured all summer long, recreating the sounds of the big bands augumented by some very unusual photographic effects on the walls and ceiling! Tommy James and The Shondells also appeared that summer, as did singer Curtis Mayfield and the group "Blood, Sweat and Tears". That great hi-de-ho man, Cab Calloway, was booked into Convention Hall, in July, with an attendance of 1,500 persons. In mid-year, the economic outlook was being described as "murky" by local business people, who said they were losing out to Cape May County resorts. And what's more, they expected it to continue unless the state got casinos.

Anthony Rey, then General Manager of the Chalfonte-Haddon Hall, stumped on television for gambling, saying it was estimated that legalized gaming could bring the state $97,000,000 a year by 1985! Incidentally, the Haddon Hall is now Resorts International, Atlantic City's first casino hotel, and Rey is now Vice President of Resorts International, Incorporated!

Senior Citizens were protesting what they called "inequitable rates" charged by Atlantic City Electric Company, while at the same time objecting to rate hikes by New Jersey Bell! Assemblyman Steven Perskie, even then with dreams of becoming the Senator from Atlantic County, was stumping to convert people to casinos. There was talk of a monorail along our boardwalk and a huge Disneyland-type attraction for the city. George A. Hamid, Jr., sold Steel Pier to Maxwell "Sonny" Goldberg and Milton Neustadter, operators of the Howard Johnson's Regency, for $1,000,000.

"Monopoly" fans were irate when Public Works Commissioner Arthur Ponzio proposed an ordinance to change the names of Baltic, Arctic and Mediterranean Avenues in the resort! Those streets appear on the Monopoly board as the cheapest areas of property in our town. Parker Brothers, owners of the game, appeared here to protest. The change never came about, and there was even talk of printing the name "Atlantic City" across the board the following year! This, too, has not happened.

We had some nice songs in '73: "Song Sung Blue", "The Summer Knows", "Speak Softly Love", "Daddy Don't You Walk So Fast", and "Where Is The Love?".

1974

Motorists may recall this year with mixed emotions. Automobiles were bigger and better but gasoline prices shot up as much as five cents a gallon, with experts predicting an even greater increase by year's end! The 55-mile-an-hour speed limit was introduced as one way of conserving fuel. The "Save NAFEC" campaign was in full swing, with petitions and bumper stickers urging that the National Aviation Facilities Experimental Center in Pomona be kept in operation for economic and safety reasons.

Michael Matthews became the first Democratic Freeholder, in this century, in Atlantic County. Early morning darkness was plaguing students and school bus drivers as the state put into effect a measure designed to save energy. Parents were up in arms, saying it was unsafe for children to stand along the roadside, waiting for the bus, in the early morning hours.

Hilton Inns was granted a franchise to build a hotel complex adjacent to Convention Hall, and believe it or not, there were complaints that winter of a shortage of snow! Seems our area escaped the snowfalls of other parts of the state and devotees of winter sports were unhappy.

Albert Zugsmith, a former resort newspaper man, who later made it big in Hollywood as a producer of motion pictures, was publicly lauding casinos as the salvation of Atlantic City. Another effort was begun to get the casino issue on the November ballot and a $1,000,000 goal was set by the campaign leaders to publicize the need for dice and wheels in New Jersey. Yes, the original idea was to make gaming legal throughout the state. However, the measure was defeated, with only two counties going for casinos! Guess which was one of them!

Political analysts bemoaned the fact that this would be the last time the casino issue would appear on the ballot for at least 10 years. So, other means of reviving our city were being sought, especially in view of the fact that Atlantic City then ranked second only to Newark in loss of business during the three-year period then drawing to a close. To give you some idea, our town had lost 9.6 per cent of its commercial properties!

There was growing concern about a nuclear power plant to be located two miles off our coast, and the U.S. Conference on the 200-mile limit favored fast action to protect fishing interests here.

Mayor Joseph Bradway announced that the city had received a $100,000 "safe streets" grant for the demolition of dilapidated buildings, primarily in the Inlet section. Vice-President Gerald Ford visited Atlantic City to address the American Farm Bureau Federation, and Margate introduced a beach fee.

The speedboat "Slapshot" won the Hennessey Gran Prix Regatta, navigating the 181-mile course with ease, in record time. A charter study movement was begun in the resort and more than a thousand persons signed the petition, which later was thrown out when many of the signatures were questioned on the basis of legality.

On the entertainment scene, singer Trini Lopez, The Dovells, and The Orlons played Steel Pier. Song stylist Arthur Prysock, and Dorothy Donegan were starring at Le Bistro.

At the movies, some outstanding offerings of the year included "Papillon", "The Sting", "Vanishing Wilderness", "The Way We Were", "The Exorcist" and "Chinatown". In May, the old Breakers Hotel on the Boardwalk at New Jersey Avenue came down, joining the Traymore Hotel in death by dynamite. It had begun life as the Rudolf in 1909 being renamed the Breakers in 1916. The hostelry was famous nationwide as *"The"* kosher hotel in Atlantic City and had played host to many of the resort's conventions year after year.

1975

The Atlantic City Beach Patrol signed up its first female lifeguard for a three-year probationary period. She was Virginia Gaye Kelly, who, in 1974, had failed her boat test. She promised she'd be back and she was! This time she passed and was accepted. Gaye, as she prefers to be called, is now a full-fledged member of the Beach Patrol, taking her place among a group of men and women who enjoy a proud heritage of service dating back to 1892, when the organization started working as a paid force.

1975 saw a great fire at the Sheraton-Deauville Hotel with damage set at $250,000! Financial experts were making dire predictions that motorists soon would be paying 90¢ a gallon for gasoline! Our city was making plans for the upcoming American Bicentennial and seeking suggestions from the public as to what could be done to make the celebration a really memorable affair. And the business community was looking eagerly forward to that time, one year hence, when the huge overflow crowds, unable to find accommodations in Philadelphia, would be coming to Atlantic City in droves. This didn't happen, however, and Philadelphia itself failed to attract the large Bicentennial throngs that were expected.

The question to be placed before the voters on the November ballot would ask the electorate to allow a charter study unit to be formed to investigate the possibilities of having a Mayor-Council system of government, which would replace the Commission form which had been adopted in May of 1912. The issue was decided at an election in 1977, with the voters indicating a preference for the present Commission system, at least for the time being.

Jitney drivers were looking for an increase of 5¢ in fares, the total amount, incidentally, which was charged for a ride when the service was first organized in 1915!

The exciting "Miss America" Powerboat Race was held that summer with some 20 sleek speedboats participating. Most all of those entered in the event were valued at $40,000 and up! At the end of the 81-mile race, a boat from Miami named "Streaker" was the winner.

Steel Pier that summer featured, among many attractions, singer Al Martino, and Billy Harner, and Good Wood, a rock group. Songstress Cleo Laine was in town for a one-night concert at the Pennsylvania Room of Haddon Hall, sponsored by the Atlantic Performing Arts Center. On local movie screens, we enjoyed "Funny Lady", "Earthquake", "Return of the Pink Panther", and "Jaws", which was not looked upon as good publicity for shore resorts!

1975 was the year we should have invested in real estate in Atlantic City. One could have purchased a brick duplex on the south side for $9,000 and another, which was advertised as being "A stone's throw from the beach", for $14,500.

The song "Feelings" made it big that year as did "I Write The Songs", "Laughter in the Rain", "Please Mr. Please", and "The Last Farewell".

1976

This was the year that was! First, it marked the 200th birthday of our nation, and Atlantic City went all out with celebrations, decorations, parades and, of course, fireworks! But the next biggest event for '76 has to be the passing of the referendum making casino gaming legal for Atlantic City! It happened on November 2, with the measure being carried by an overwhelming majority around the state!

Two years earlier, the question had gone down to defeat and it was just about a foregone conclusion that it was a dead issue for at least 10 years. But two lawmakers got their heads together and devised a plan which they thought just might work. They were Atlantic County Assemblyman Steven Perskie and Atlantic County Senator Joseph McGahn, two Democrats with one idea . . . Atlantic City must have casinos to survive! They were in agreement that the question of legalized gaming should again be put before the voters, as it had in 1974, but this time, make it for Atlantic City only!

So a bill was drawn up to get this differently-worded question on the November ballot. Legislators in Trenton liked the idea and so did the voters. The night it passed, I was covering the election for WFPG from one of our remote locations, the Haddon Hall Hotel, which ironically, would become Atlantic City's and the east coast's first casino!

As the votes were tabulated, we slowly realized that this time, it looked like it would make it, with votes to spare. And it did, with just about every county going for casinos, so long as they were kept in Atlantic City! As I walked back to the studio along a dark and deserted boardwalk that night, I had a strange sensation of having witnessed history in the making, and that our town was on the brink of something big. But I had mixed emotions. I loved the old Atlantic City and I was aware that some of it would have to go to make way for those dazzling new casinos of the future!

In other news that year, the Concorde SST Jetliner was rumored to be landing at NAFEC, if plans worked out. Mayor Joseph Bradway was saying the SST should use NAFEC for a one-year trial period, but there was opposition because of the noise of the big plane. A beautification project for the Northside was initiated by Cora Boggs, called "Guild the Ghetto". And our city became free of the controversial "jam joints" after a 10-year battle. The last one on the boardwalk was closed that summer.

The "Sunshine Law" took effect in Atlantic City and throughout the state and was first used on January 19. A local U.F.O. sighting was in the news when Atlantic City Press columnist "Sonny" Schwartz and Ventnor City Police Patrolman Frank Ingargiola spotted a strange craft in the night skies. They drove along the boardwalk watching the object in awe and amazement. The two men swear they know what they saw, but authorities discounted the sighting, saying it was merely the reflection of light from a boat on a low-hanging cloud!

The first instance of a church's conversion into an entertainment spot occurred in 1976, when Olivet Presbyterian Church, Tennessee and Pacific Avenues, was renovated and later that year opened as

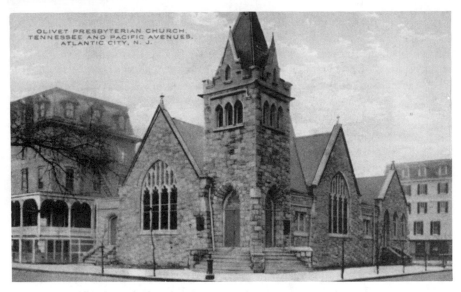

Pub. by the Post Card Distributing Company, Atlantic City, N.J.

Littlejohn's, which has become a mecca for pleasure-seekers. The structure's exterior was not disturbed, and little of the interior was changed, except to make the pews shorter and change their location. Even the stained-glass windows were retained.

The motion picture, "The Hindenburg", made movie history, and as the year drew to a close, the colorful celebrations marking the nation's Bicentennial were winding down but hundreds of people had happy memories of the largest beach party ever held, the kite-flying contest on the beach, and the "Escape to Atlantic City" weekend that January!

"C.R.A.C.", the Committee to Rebuild Atlantic City, which had been organized to get out the vote for casinos, could look back on a job well done, with so many people pitching in to do their part. Sanford Weiner, the man hired as head honcho for the project, left town with the sweet smell of success in his nostrils.

And, oh yes. Television viewers no longer had to watch those "Bicentennial Minutes"!

1977

We began gearing up for the casino era and Resorts International's President I. G. "Jack" Davis was saying his firm had, on standby, about 150 pit bosses and other casino workers, ready to train local residents for future jobs in their new casino in the Haddon Hall Hotel. The new owners planned to re-name it "The Palace", but due to public displeasure they reconsidered and decided to call it Resorts International after the parent company, adding that it would remain Resorts International forever! Stock in the firm was selling for about $18 a share in 1977. But did you buy any, and if so, why did you sell it so soon?

The town was packed for the July 4th weekend with 45,000 arriving vehicles clocked during a 14-hour period! The square-rigged sailing ship "Enchantress", captained by David Kent, arrived at Gardner's Basin where she would be used to carry passengers on sight-seeing cruises along the coast. Proponents of our rolling chairs were saying casinos would increase the popularity of the colorful conveyances, due to the influx of people who had never even seen one.

Young Bruce Condella broke the world's pinball record at Steel Pier, when he played for 92 hours, 44 minutes, to get his name in the Guiness Book of World Records! The 18-year old was on the verge of collapse following his feat. And Mayor Joseph Lazarow, got himself entered in the same book by establishing a new record for hand-shaking, that summer. The hand was bruised and swollen after he had exchanged greetings with 11,030 persons, but he broke the record set early in the century by President Theodore Roosevelt!

Incumbent Governor Brendan Byrne and the man who wanted to replace him, Senator Raymond Bateman, debated at Howard Johnson's Regency. Angelos Demetriou promised that his master plan would not disrupt the ethnic character of our neighborhoods, either by zoning changes or condemnation of housing.

Sea-clammers were staying ashore in a dispute based on the fact they were being paid only $4 per bushel as compared to $9 the previous years. WFPG's vice president and general manager Cathy Clark became the first woman president of the New Jersey Broadcasters Association. And the long-time Republican leader of Atlantic County, Senator Frank S. "Hap" Farley died in his sleep in September following a long illness.

Come summer and the singing team of England Dan and John Ford Coley starred on Steel Pier and area residents were flocking to NAFEC in Pomona, for Transfair '77, a gigantic transportation expositon. In December a disastrous fire on the Boardwalk between New York Avenue and St. James Place, resulted in $750,000 damage! And, as the year drew to a close, the first Atlantic City meeting of the newly-created Casino Control Commission was held in Convention Hall.

Popular songs included "The Wreck of the Edmund Fitzgerald", "Paloma Blanca", "After the Lovin' ", "Save Your Kisses For Me" and "Fernando".

1978

The word was that Atlantic City's first legal casino, Resorts International, would be in operation by Memorial Day, and they made it! On May 26th, people were standing in lines on the Boardwalk at North Carolina Avenue waiting for the doors to open! I chatted with a number of them from many parts of the country as they stood patiently awaiting this long-promised opportunity to try their luck at the slots and tables without traveling to Nevada.

Entertainer Steve Lawrence played the first craps game with Mayor Lazarow. Governor Byrne was there to cut the ribbon. Following its first full month of operation, the casino's Board Chairman James Crosby announced the June "win" was $16,000,000!

Jack Freeman, Inc., Longport, N. J.

Caesar's World won out over Penthouse in a bid to secure the Howard Johnson's Regency and it became Atlantic City's second casino, in 1979. Oil exploration off our coast, in the Baltimore Canyon trough began, and two men died in the crash of a helicopter flying to a drilling rig offshore.

Local attorney Gerald Weinstein won a four-year battle to be named Atlantic County Court Judge. Catherine Cramer cancelled her popular Pro-Am Bicycle Race, which for two years had attracted top names in the sport, following a dispute with the city fathers over funding. The event was snapped up the same year by the city of Wildwood.

The Planning Board approved the moving of the controversial World War monument at the entrance to the city, into the adjoining park but as of now, it remains where it has stood since 1923! County Prosecutor Richard Williams was saying crime would go up 78% by 1982, due to casinos and an increase in population. Rumors were flying that Steel Pier had been sold to a Philadelphia developer for $6,000,000, but the truth was that it was sold, later in the year, to Resorts International for $3,800,000 in company stock!

This proved to be the last year for the big pier as an amusement center, and the "Fabulous High-Diving Horse" made his daring leap for the last time in lack-lustre surroundings and before a sparse crowd. I witnessed one of those final performances and my memory raced back to the time when thousands sat enthralled and one could almost hear a pin drop as the animal stood poised, at the top of the ladder, deciding on the proper moment to jump. At this writing, Resorts has announced no definite plans for the former showplace, which was major attraction for 80 years.

A howling blizzard struck the city on February 6, leaving 13 inches of snow, which closed all schools, most businesses and paralyzed traffic! Beach erosion was the most damaging in years.

C. T. Art-Colortone. Made only by Curt Teich & Co., Inc. Chicago, U.S.A.

Early in July, a "Red Tide" was spotted off our shores, an algae growth, which, fortunately proved harmless. Disc Jockey Ed Hurst rang down the curtain on the final show of his popular "Summertime On The Pier", a series which had been on Philadelphia television since 1959! A highlight of his shows were the fashion parades of lovely models, with Marie McCullough as commentator.

Benihana of Tokyo, the restaurant chain, was looking to buy the Shelburne Hotel, for a proposed $35,000,000 casino complex. Playboy Enterprises received conditional approval for its $36,000,000 casino next to Convention Hall, as residents continued to marvel at the astronomical figures being tossed around!

Parking meters were installed at the city's airport, Bader Field, a source of revenue which had gone untapped all those years! Lit's Department store, at South Carolina and Atlantic, was purchased by Senator Steven Perskie and a Philadelphia businessman for conversion to offices. Later in the year, Golden Nugget bought a block of Atlantic City property between Pennsylvania and Virginia Avenues, for a proposed casino, and the Ritz Apartments was purchased for conversion into a casino complex, for $11,000,000.

City officials took exception to an announcement prior to the Memorial Day weekend by State Police Superintendent Clinton Pagano, that traffic in the city would be so heavy he was considering issuing orders to turn motorists away. His fears proved groundless, however, and traffic created no problems. As I recall, the weather was a factor, since it was not what one could call a perfect seashore weekend.

This was the year many business analysts consider to be the turning point for Atlantic City, putting it back into the running as one of the nation's premier resorts. Then there were those who did not agree, saying it would require more than casinos to bring about a return of the glory days here, in what had been known for decades, as "The World's Playground".

1979

Early in the year, Elvis Presley's '55 Corvette was sold for $34,500 at the annual Antique Auto Auction, in Convention Hall! We were really shivering, too, with the mercury hovering at or near the zero mark in February, for quite a few days. And to make things worse, we were battered by a blizzard that month with snow up to two feet deep in many places!

The casino era was really gathering momentum, with Resorts International still the only game in town! Card-counters came under fire from Resorts' management, and the counters complained bitterly saying they were doing nothing wrong. But the big casino banished them from the premises and the Casino Control Commission agreed. R-I's January "win" dropped by 8% from December, but still was 'way ahead of Las Vegas!

A Swedish steamship company, Stenna Lines, was contemplating construction of a floating casino-hotel in the Marina area. Economist Frederick Hayes said that by 1980, Atlantic casinos could possibly have an annual win of between $1,000,000,000 and $1,500,000,000!

The annual March of Dimes Telethon set a new record of $118,333! A gasoline shortage, which many motorists thought was contrived, was causing long lines at the pumps! Caesar's and Bally were vying for the honor of opening the city's second gaming hall. Then suddenly it was June 26, and the beautiful Caesar's Boardwalk Regency opened in the former Howard Johnson's property, on the 'walk at Arkansas Avenue! The opening attraction was Paul Anka . Other big names, appearing at the new showplace in its premier season, included Bob Newhart, Marty Allen, Rich Little, and Neil Sedaka.

The gasoline crunch was dealing a knockout punch to resort business, including motels and other facilities along the highways leading to the resort. Hotels in the city, including the town's lone casino, did well Memorial Day weekend, but merchants were saying business was off by about 20% due to cold weather and the gasoline crunch.

The Atlantic City Jazz Festival was held at Gardner's Basin, in July, with a roster of top stars in person: Nancy Wilson, Roy Ayars, Herbie Mann, Sarah Vaughan, Lonnie Liston Smith, Mongo Santa Maria, Billy Eckstein, Earl "Fatha" Hines, Buddy Rich and Maynard Ferguson and their orchestras.

Frank Sinatra was in town at Resorts International, recalling his early days at the Steel Pier as vocalist with Tommy Dorsey's Band, and Harry James Orchestra.

Resorts International took over operation of the Boardwalk Trams, and a charter study plan for our town was okayed by the Greater Atlantic City Chamber of Commerce, with the University of Pennsylvania supplying the personnel. Condominium conversion was causing concern for many apartment dwellers and Mayor Lazarow went to bat for them, with

City Commission instituting a one-year moratorium on the practice.

A forecast by an organization called Economic Research Associates predicted 26 casinos here by 1990, a population of 75,000 as compared to our present 42,600, more than 18,000,000 visitors annually by 1985, and more than 24,000,000 by 1990! It also forecast 276,000 casino jobs by 1990, with a need for almost 55,000 hotel rooms and 7,700 additional housing units! The full story appears in the Press of Atlantic City for November 16, 1979. It further stated that 7,500,000 visitors would come to see us in 1980!

The finale for Steel Pier, as we knew it, became most apparent when an auction sale of memorabilia from the old amusement center was held in, of all places, Monroeville, in Salem County, some 50 miles away! There were signs, grotesque characters from the fun houses, animals which had been on display, loudspeakers once used to announce the high diving horses and other spectacles in the water sports show and marine carnival. My good friend, Jack Montez, had been the announcer out there at the end of the pier from 1936 to 1965, when he retired. Montez passed on in 1978.

At the same auction, artifacts from the old Haddon Hall Hotel went on the block, due to the fact that that building, like Steel Pier, had undergone some startling changes and was slated for demolition. Prices were reported to be very fair, by people looking for such memorabilia, and they realized they had a few pieces of history!

Prices continued to soar for just about everything we bought! The new Mercury automobiles were now tagged at $6,549, and a new Ford had a sticker price of $6,995. At the store, we were paying 79¢ a pound for smoked hams; $1.99 a pound for top of the round; and $1.79 for pork chops.

Our music has changed over the years, but it still plays a major role in the life of Atlantic City, and some of '79's hits included "Sad Eyes", "Still", "My Sharona", "Rise" and "Enough Is Enough" (No More Tears).

The year ended on a high note, with the city's third casino, Bally's plush "Park Place" Casino Hotel opening on December 29, to the acclaim of thousands who were amazed at what had replaced an equally plush hotel of another era, the Marlborough-Blenheim. The opening attraction at Park Place was the team of Marilyn McCoo and Billy Davis, Jr.

EPILOGUE

Well, here it is . . . five years later . . . as I sit down to update my "Atlantic City Diary" in September of 1985. The original edition ended with 1980 and three hotel casinos in operation. Now we have 11. Not too much else has happened in Atlantic City, except that many more fine old landmarks have fallen to the wreckers' ball, including a few which were on the official list of Historic Places. For all intents and purposes, they were to have been preserved, but efforts by people dedicated to this end proved futile.

Our government has changed, but the monument in the middle of the street still is where it has been since 1923, despite continuing efforts by some factions to have it moved. Our convention business has had its ups and downs because of lack of sufficient hotel rooms, but it appears this problem will soon be remedied with the construction of a number of non-casino hotels on the Black Horse and White Horse Pikes.

I've changed radio stations. After 37 years with WFPG/WIIN, I joined WMID-NBC in Atlantic City in October of 1983 where I play the music of the 1930s, 1940s, and 1950s, concentrating on the big bands, between 6 and 10 AM, Monday through Friday, and I LOVE IT! I'm actually playing the music on records I introduced on the air as a young staff announcer when I began my career in this town in 1946. And I brought my daily Atlantic City history program "Through the Rear View Mirror" along with me, with the same loyal sponsor, Siracusa Real Estate and Insurance Company.

1980

Atlantic City's fourth hotel casino, the Brighton opened on August 13, carrying on a proud old name. Ironically, the former Brighton Hotel, dating back to the late 1870s, advertised itself as the Brighton "Casino", although no gambling took place there, legally at least, so far as we can learn. In 1959, the old building was razed and the ultra-modern Colony Motel was built on the site. With the opening of the Brighton Hotel Casino, historians applauded the decision to perpetuate the name, but within a year or so, it was renamed The Sands. For awhile, its music director was the famous trombonist-bandleader Si Zentner, formerly with Resorts.

Before the year was over, we had two more gaming halls: Harrah's Marina Hotel Casino which opened November 20, and the Golden Nugget which began operation on December 13. Harrah's was the first such facility to open away from the Boardwalk where the others were concentrated. In fact, their advertising continues to describe their location as "The Other Atlantic City." It's near the approach to the Brigantine Bridge, in the Marina section of town on Brigantine Boulevard. The Nugget, as it is familiarly known, stands on the site of Manny Solomon's former Strand Motel on the 'walk at Boston Avenue.

Atlantic County Senator Steven Perskie took the city to task, zeroing in on the business community, urging it to shape up, if it was to be successful and make the most of the impact of the casino era. A new "clean streets" program was launched by the city administration, featuring new 80-gallon trash containers on wheels. Public Works Commissioner Joseph Pasquale said he had 300 such units for distribution to selected homes in the Venice Park and Chelsea Heights sections.

The controversial issue of the proposed closing of Bader Field Airport surfaced again with local activist brothers John and Joseph Polillo taking the position that preservation of the facility would pose no problem for adjacent neighborhoods and would insure their remaining intact.

Our Mayor in 1980 was Joseph Lazarow and our Police Chief was Joseph Allmond. Both men had their work cut out for them, but handled their jobs well and weathered the storm. Al Rosen, former President of the

New York Yankees, resigned as Executive Vice-President of Bally's Park Place Hotel Casino after 15 months in that capacity. Speaking of Bally's, they were offering a real good deal to attract customers. For 75¢, one could board a casino bus in Northeast Philadelphia, Baltimore, Washington, or New York and travel to Atlantic City where each passenger received a $10 roll of quarters, no strings attached!

At this writing, the long-awaited rail link between Atlantic City and Philadelphia seems to be within our grasp, thanks to the hard work of local politicos and business people, and a Federal grant of $30,000,000. But as far back as 1980, the project had been given second priority in the nation by the U.S. Department of Transportation for Amtrak. New Jersey Representative James Florio was saying the service could be in operation "within 3 years", carrying passengers to the shore in less than 50 minutes at speeds up to 79 miles an hour! At that time, several Japanese and French firms expressed interest in the project.

Food prices in 1980 seem quite reasonable compared with today. Thriftway on Absecon Boulevard advertised sirloin steaks at $2.19 a pound; apples at 3 pounds for 89¢ and Coke or Tab, 99¢ for a 2-litre bottle. Local newspaper ads offered apartment rentals ranging from $250 to $400 per month. City Commissioner Edmund Colanzi pronounced his "City Hall on the Move" program a success during the 10-week period in which Colanzi visited just about every neighborhood seeking input from residents concerning problems and possible solutions.

I lost a dear friend in 1980, a man with whom I had worked in radio in the 1950s. He was Al Owen who arrived in the resort to help put Station WMID on the air in 1947. Al had been a personality at Detroit's WXYZ, announcing on the network for such shows as "The Green Hornet" and "Yukon King". As Program Director for WMID, Owen introduced many innovations on the local airwaves. His was the first talk program with celebrity interviews to originate at pool side at the old Brighton and Chelsea Hotels among others. Later in his career, he came to WFPG where we worked together for some time, when he hosted the afternoon drive time record show "Million Dollar Ballroom." His program's theme was Ray Anthony's recording of "The Man With the Horn" and Al often sang along with the records. Leaving radio, Owen later served as Executive Director of the Greater Atlantic City Chamber of Commerce and as Public Relations Director for the City of Atlantic City. Al passed on suddenly, of a heart attack. His death was a shock to his host of friends and associates. As I write this, I recall how enthusiastic Al was about the casinos. If ever there was a person ready for these exciting times in our town, it was Al Owen. When he and I announced for the name bands from Steel Pier . . . he for the Mutual Radio Network and I for the American Broadcasting Company . . . we never dreamed Atlantic City would someday become the entertainment mecca of the East. Rest in peace, Al.

As 1980 drew to a close, our skyline continued to change, with six casinos going full blast. During the year, our town had played host to 13,822,000 persons, 3,298,000 of whom had arrived by charter bus. Total industry payroll for the casinos in 1980 amounted to almost

$268,000,000, and employment at our hotel casinos and related businesses was increasing by leaps and bounds. Waiting in the wings were three more gaming houses, as the populace continued to wonder if we would have 26 casinos by the year 1990, as had been predicted in 1979 by an organization called Economic Research Association. Only time will tell!

1981

Reasonably priced airfares to Florida have been blamed in part for the decline of Atlantic City as a tourist resort, starting back in the fifties. People figured that, for a few dollars more, they could fly to Florida instead of coming here. This included many conventions as well as individuals. It was a surprise therefore, when in 1981, Atlantic International Airline was the first to plan regularly scheduled package tours to Atlantic City and was advertising 21 weekly flights to the Federal Aviation Technical Center in Pomona, where our municipal airport is located. Actually, it's quite a distance from Atlantic City, on the site of the former U.S. Naval Air Station which played a major role in the Second World War. AIA continued service for quite awhile, but eventually threw in the towel.

We saw three new hotel casino openings in 1981. Elsinore's Playboy was first, on April 14. The Claridge was next, opening on July 20. On November 23, the Tropicana Hotel Casino opened on the site of the old Ambassador Hotel, "The Monarch of the Boardwalk." This gave us nine gaming halls. Playboy and the "Trop" are new from the ground up, while the Claridge retains not only the original name but much of the original structure. It was the last great Boardwalk hotel to be built, opening on December 17, 1930. Much of its plush interior was integrated into the new design and decor of the hotel casino, harking back to an earlier day when life moved at a slower pace.

Then, as now, casino operators were complaining of over-regulation by the Casino Control Commission and Chairman Joseph Lordi promised a sweeping review of the rules. And the question remained: why was the Commission based in Lawrenceville, rather than in Atlantic City? An effort is now being made to move the panel here. The fledging industry was making news not only in New Jersey but out in Nevada too, where competition from our casinos was making an impact.

City Commissioner Michael Matthews, a Democrat who would become our Mayor in 1982, sponsored a study to see whether the city really did need more police officers. The administration was saying we needed about 130 additional personnel. Police Chief Joseph Allmond, Public Safety Commissioner Willie Clayton, and Matthews opposed the idea. The public, of course, was very much in favor of hiring as many more officers as possible.

State officials granted Atlantic Electric Company permission to convert two oil-fired generators to coal which the company said could result in savings of $30,000,000 by 1984. In sports, the Atlantic City Hi-Rollers of the Continental Basketball Association defeated the Montana

Golden Nuggets 119-116 at the Westside Complex in January. The new Oldsmobile Cutlass Supreme coupe carried a sticker price of $7,899 and car buyers were wondering when prices would level off. Speaking of prices, householders were paying $1.29 for pork chops; 37¢ a pound for apples; $1.59 for a half pound of Swiss cheese; and $1.16 for a 12-ounce can of Spam.

The 14th Around-Absecon Island Swim that July was won by defending champion Paul Asmuth of Arizona State University. There was a field of 19 swimmers. Asmuth's time for the gruelling 22-mile course was 8 hours, 49 minutes, 30 seconds, finishing 35 minutes in front of his nearest competitor.

For the first time since WFPG-TV signed off on Channel 46 in May, 1954, after 19 months as Atlantic City's first commercial television station, the resort again had a TV outlet when WWAC-TV went on the air in July in the former Acme Supermarket at Connecticut and Atlantic Avenues. The station went to black less than a year later because of financial difficulties and other problems. Some of the personalities you may remember having seen on Channel 53 include Program Director Calvin Iszard; News Director Mike Crowley; News Reporter Nora Muchanic; Weather Reporter Lynn Weidner, who also doubled in news; Entertainment Reporter John Frasier; and News Anchorman, bearded, jovial James G. Knight.

Baseball fans were excited over the news that Resorts International Hotel Casino had signed Mike Schmidt, Garry Maddox, and Larry Bowa, stars of the World Champion Philadelphia Phillies, to appear in the Green Room there, for autograph sessions. And almost 2500 bicyclists converged on our town on Sunday, July 26, in the 62-mile run from Philadelphia in the American Cancer Society's annual Bike-a-Thon.

City Commissioner Joseph Pasquale unveiled a $15,500,000 Capital Improvements program. The salaries of Mayor Joseph Lazarow and the City Commissioners were raised by 27%. The Mayor's pay went from $31,000 to $39,000 a year, while those of Commissioners Clayton, Colanzi, Pasquale, and Matthews increased from $27,500 to $35,000.

Popular television programs of the day included "Eight is Enough"; "Soap"; "Mork and Mindy"; "It's a Living"; and "Breaking Away". Ice Capades still played Atlantic City's Convention Hall each summer with seats now going for $6, $7, and $8. Many of our readers can remember when those same seats could be had for $2, $3, and $4 with General Admission seating as low as $1! The dazzling ice revue always played here prior to Pittsburgh and was one of the highlights of our Summer season. It has since left town permanently and we miss it. Somehow, it just doesn't seem like Summer without Ice Capades.

Resorts International stock was listed in the $25-$28 range early in 1981 and continued to go up. The Salvation Army Citadel on Texas Avenue was attracting more and more stranded travelers and helped as many as it possibly could. Captain David Crawford was in charge of the facility, and somehow, kept smiling in spite of a heavy schedule.

At year's end, we noted that 191,065 charter buses had brought 5,918,466 passengers into Atlantic City, up quite a bit compared to 1980.

And so was the payroll of the hotel casino industry. It amounted to a whopping $464,368,775, an increase of more than $196,000,000 compared with the previous year. And we were seeing more and more people on our streets, wearing the now-familiar "uniforms" of the casino dealers. Traffic caused headaches for our Police Department, especially on weekends and holidays. But motorists were finding parking lot rates more to their liking now, following a period in which the cost was almost prohibitive for those having to come into the city daily for work or business.

1982

After 70 years under the Commission form of government, Atlantic City went Councilmanic in 1982 as voters decided the change just might make a difference. Democratic Commissioner Michael Matthews won the election for Mayor, but the relationship between Council and the new Mayor seemed doomed from the start. There were differences of opinion from the outset and, try as they might, each side failed to achieve any kind of unity. Believe it or not, separate inaugural ceremonies were held in July. Matthews' predecessor, Republican Joseph Lazarow had held the post six years.

The casino era rolled on with Donald Trump taking Holiday Inns as a partner for his new Atlantic City operation. Trump Plaza on the Boardwalk near Convention Hall would become our 10th hotel casino, but not for at least two years. Even then, legislators were trying to get 24-hour gaming in Atlantic City with Mayor Matthews, also a State Assemblyman, spearheading the effort in Trenton. Under state law, casinos must close between 4 AM and 10 AM weekdays and 6 AM and 10 AM on weekends and holidays. At this writing, the 24-hour gaming idea refuses to die, with proponents saying it would eliminate the traffic tie-ups which occur when all the casinos close at the same time. If they were open around the clock, departures would be staggered, resulting in a smoother flow of traffic. At present, when the mass exodus occurs, all three main roads out of the resort are jammed.

Popular television shows included "Different Strokes"; "Barney Miller"; "My Old Man"; "Fame"; and "Hill Street Blues". The 1982 Pontiac hatchback T-1000 was selling for $5,595 delivered, at Kerbeck in Atlantic City. The "Press" was offering free classified ads called "Freebies". Remember that cute little bumble bee logo? The famous Club Harlem on North Kentucky Avenue, our oldest night club still in existence opened for its 48th season with HI-FI White on stage.

The Tropicana Hotel Casino sponsored a free concert on the beach at Iowa Avenue with the theme "Hooked on Classics" with music under the direction of Louis Clark. Thousands of music lovers came to enjoy the event. Casino showrooms continued trying to outshine each other by offering the public top talent. Caesar's featured Rich Little; Eddie Fisher was at The Claridge; The Sands had Bernadette Peters, Joel Gray, Linda Carter, and Shirley MacLaine, among others. At The Golden Nugget, a revue called "Follies On Broadway" was a popular attraction. Atlantic

City continued to resist the temptation to establish a beach fee, even though almost all of the resorts up and down the coast have one. Down beach, Lucy the Margate elephant celebrated her 100th birthday all year long with lots of special events. The unique structure was built as a real estate attraction . . . one of three, and the only one to survive the ravages of time and weather.

Gardner's Basin Maritime Park in the Inlet continued its valiant efforts to become a major attraction with the schooner "Flying Cloud" on exhibit, twice-daily sailings of the bark "Young America" along the coast and the gala "Harborfest" in mid-Summer, but visitors dwindled in number. Reasons given for the apparent lack of interest range from its location to lack of public relations and advertising. At one time, our Inlet was one of the nicest sections of town with lovely homes, well-kept lawns and friendly neighborhoods. Over the years, it has fallen on bad times, and today is shunned by visitors and residents alike except by those who live there and remain loyal to their part of the city. They continue to hold out hope that it will be rebuilt and it appears they may be right, because construction is beginning there and once this takes hold, more and more investors may follow suit.

Birds Eye View, Showing Inlet. Atlantic City, N. J.

The "win" at Atlantic City's nine casinos for December, 1982, was quite healthy. Resorts International led the pack with $16.3 million; Bally's Park Place was second with $16.1 million, and Caesar's was next with a win of $14.3 million. Harrah's Marina was in fourth place with a win of $12.3 million; then came Tropicana with $11.2 million; Sands with $10.2, Playboy, $9.4; Golden Nugget, $8.5; and Claridge with $6.3 million. All nine combined won a total $1,500,000,000 (yes, that's with a "B") in 1982 with gamblers losing about $4,000,000 a day. This represented an increase in win of more than 35 percent compared to 1981 which saw a win of $1.1 billion. To explain the term "win": The gross win should not be confused with profit. It is the amount won from patrons before taxes, wages, fringe benefits, debt services and other expenses are deducted.

Buses bringing in thousands of day-trippers continued to rile residents who charged they were adversely affected by fumes and noise. As a result, lots outside the city proper began to spring up on the Black Horse and White Horse Pikes, including one owned by an automobile dealership on Albany Avenue. Going rate for bus parking is in the neighborhood of $13 per day.

Atlantic City was even more popular as a tourist destination in 1982. According to the report prepared by the Atlantic City Casino Association with information supplied by the New Jersey Expressway Authority, 13,086,000 persons arrived here in private vehicles. Another 9,051,000 came via chartered bus. Franchise buses transported 595,000 people to our town and 223,000 more flew in. The first year for casino air charters was 1981, when AIA initiated service. The casino industry listed salaries, including fringe benefits and payroll expenses as $563,210,193 for the total number of gaming halls in the city.

For the first time in four years, when our first hotel casino, Resorts International opened in May of 1978, there were no new ones built in 1982, nor would there be any more till 1984 when Trump Plaza would open. It seemed that the initial excitement had subsided, at least for the present, and potential investors were taking a long, hard look at our existing casinos before deciding to begin construction.

The 1980 census shows Atlantic City with a population of 40,199. The 1990 projection is 42,892, this despite the fact that the exodus to the Mainland continues. It was not so long ago that we had a population close to 45,000. As of December, 1982, employment in the casino industry was approximately 28,800 and going up. This did not include support industries.

Old landmarks continued to disappear almost overnight and many's the person who wondered what had happened to that shop or store, that restaurant or an old corner bar where they had enjoyed hoisting a cold one on a hot summer's day long ago. It was all happening in the name of progress but old timers sadly shook their heads, wondering if those in charge of all the changes knew what they were doing.

The drawbridge on Albany Avenue at the entrance to the city over Beach Thorofare was dedicated on October 14 as the Peter Egnor Memorial Bridge in honor of the brave and popular Atlantic City police officer killed in the line of duty in a shootout. County Senator Steven Perskie had sponsored the proposal.

A part of our past for millions of people, including me, went up in smoke and flames on the cold, grey morning of December 10, 1982, when Steel Pier burned to the decking. Suspected cause was arson. It went fast, and when the fire was over, the once-famous "Showplace of the Nation" lay in ruins. Radio stations WIIN/WFPG had moved from the premises it had occupied since 1940, in 1982, relocating at California and Atlantic Avenues. The Pier's owners, Resorts International, are now rebuilding the pier, and when it's finished, Steel Pier will live again and we hope, become the mecca for fun-lovers and entertainment seekers that it had been since it opened in 1898. For me, the Pier was never the same after the Marine Ballroom was destroyed by in 1969.

1983

The famous singing group "The Beach Boys" gave a free concert on our beach, sponsored by Caesar's Hotel Casino on July 3 with approximately 200,000 persons in attendance. No problems developed, despite dire predictions by U. S. Interior Secretary James Watt that the show was certain to attract undesirable elements. The night before, a "Fabulous Fifties Philadelphia Jamboree" was sponsored by Bally's Park Place Hotel Casino featuring the popular disc-jockey team of Joe Grady and Ed Hurst of WPEN's "950 Club" fame on hand.

The nation lost another music great in 1983 when trumpet-playing bandleader Harry James died of cancer at the age of 67. He had played in Atlantic City many times, the first of which was with his new band in 1939 in the Marine Ballroom of Steel Pier, with a young Frank Sinatra as his boy singer. And even before that, James had been here as a sideman with Goodman and other name bands.

Anthony Rey was named Senior Vice-President of Community Relations by Resorts International Incorporated. Rey had started out in the hotel business as an assistant head waiter. He had served as assistant to the famed Oscar of the Waldorf at that prestigious New York hostelry, then went on to the Astor as Vice-President and General Manager. In 1965, Rey arrived in our town to run the Chalfonte-Haddon Hall Hotel for the Leeds Lippincott Company and was asked to stay on when that fine old hotel was sold to Resorts International to become our first casino. The Chalfonte has been torn down but the Haddon Hall remains, basically unchanged, one of only three Boardwalk hotels from the pre-casino days.

Governor Thomas Kean toured the Inlet with civic leader James Usry and a group of movers and shakers and said he was "distressed" by what he saw. Kean announced a $75,000 grant to help our city's Summer Youth Employment Program. Ruffu Ford Island advertised the new Ford Escort at $5,799 and the Thunderbird at $9,799. The 16th Around-Absecon Island Swim with a field of 16 entries was held in July from Gardner's Basin and back with $34,500 in prize money up for grabs. The hands-down favorite was 25-year old Paul Asmuth and he didn't let his fans down, winning the 22½ mile event for the 4th consecutive year.

At first, the sight of hot dog carts on our streets was more of a novelty than anything else. Philadelphians and New Yorkers were used to them but it had been years since our town had them. In 1983, they suddenly appeared at sites near the casinos. The so-called "hot dog wars" erupted from time to time between the city and the vendors, as well as among the vendors themselves, vying for choice locations.

The Convention Hall Authority was formed, made up of Reginald Weekes, Dennis Beiderman, Tom Sykes, William Downey, Peter Boynton, Murray Raphel, and Albert Gardner. Their goal was to get the big hall's renovation underway. The project is near completion at this writing. Two big changes affected not only Atlantic City but the entire state as well. The New Jersey Sales Tax went up to 6% and the legal drinking age was increased to 21, effective January 1, 1983. The Trop One Club, sponsored by the Tropicana Hotel Casino was introduced and became an immediate sensation with its fantastic offers.

Atlantic City Police Sergeant Henry Madamba, a 12-year veteran of the force was named "Officer of the Year." The 34-year old Vietnam veteran was assigned to the 4 PM to Midnight shift in the Inlet and was honored for his outstanding service and devotion to duty. The average price of gasoline, including all grades with services and taxes was $1.20.5 per gallon. Fifteen-year-old Gregory Egnor, a graduate of Our Lady Star of the Sea School, attended the Boy Scout Jamboree in Canada that summer. The son of Joseph and Sandy McLaughlin, he was Troop Chaplain and held Life rank.

Pierre Hollingsworth was installed as President of the Atlantic City NAACP at St. James A.M.E. Church for another term and was lauded for his work and dedication on behalf of the civil rights group. Pageant Week was rescheduled to one week later. Traditionally, it had been held during the week starting the day after Labor Day with the Boardwalk parade. Twenty-thousand persons attended the China and Glass Show at Convention Hall and show manager William Little said it would remain here indefinitely. Now it appears we've lost the show to another city for a number of reasons, the foremost being lack of hotel rooms. Atlantic City Mayor Michael Matthews received a new Buick Electra Park Avenue sedan to drive. The vehicle cost $15,757.94. MGM Grand Hotels Incorporated closed its local office but said it planned to "keep in touch" with Atlantic City.

The casinos were being urged to get involved in the proposed rail link between Atlantic City and Philadelphia, via Lindenwold. This from State Transportation Commissioner John Sheridan who said the gaming houses would be called on to contribute millions of dollars to help make the dream become a reality, adding that they would benefit in the long run. AIA was advertising flights out of Atlantic City International Airport to Detroit for $213.78; to Cleveland for $195.78 and to Boston for $186.

Atlantic City's first motel, John's Motel at Sovereign and Pacific Avenues, closed in the face of increasing competition after 30 years. Frances Ginetti and her late husband, John had opened it in 1953 when such a venture was considered quite risky. But the Ginettis had faith and made a success of the business. Murray Fredericks, then our City Solicitor was the man who spearheaded the motel ordinance adopted in January, 1953, and Mayor Joseph Altman called motels a boon to our economy. Former theatre man Max Chasens and his wife Sylvia launched a battle to see that grandparents nationwide were granted the right of visitation with their grandchildren, regardless of the wishes of the parents and the Chasens appeared on national TV including "Donahue" to further their cause.

Another year passed with no new casino development but the 9 we had, enjoyed a banner year. In 1983, 340,248 Casino charter buses brought 10,970,551 passengers to town, up by almost 2,000,000 compared to 1982. Joseph P. Lordi, first Chairman of the Casino Control Commission, passed away in 1983 after leading the industry through its trying formative years.

Folks visiting our Boardwalk for the first time in a couple of years, or the first time ever, were surprised to see what appears to be a huge cruise ship tied up at the Boardwalk at Arkansas Avenue. The structure is actually a multi-million dollar shopping mall called "Ocean One", built on the site of the old Hamid's Million Dollar Pier. The complex houses 130 shops and other attractions on three decks. Ocean One, reminding old timers that Captain John Young's residence on the Pier was known as "Number One, Atlantic Ocean", opened in the Spring of '83 when a large replica of a champagne bottle was smashed across its "bow" as hundreds of balloons were sent aloft. Soundra Usry, now Public Relations Director for the city and I broadcast that spectacular event.

1984

The big story of 1984 in Atlantic City has to be the conviction and sentencing of Mayor Michael Matthews on conspiracy charges. Ousted by recall, Matthews later was charged with accepting a cash bribe during a "sting" operation set up by the F.B.I. The 51-year old Matthews is now serving a 15-year term at the Federal Prison in Segoville, Texas. Earlier in the year, educator James Usry announced his candidacy for Mayor in the March recall election to unseat Matthews. Usry had lost to Matthews in the 1982 election by a mere 359 votes. This time out, it was a different story and James Usry became Atlantic City's first black mayor. His opponents were Matthews and John Polillo.

Atlantic City lost one of its top boosters and I lost another good friend in February when fashion expert Marie McCullough passed on, following a long illness. Known as "The First Lady of Fashion", Marie had founded the model agency bearing her name, in 1946. Marie and I worked together on radio from the late 1940s till about 1978 on just about every Miss America Pageant parade, from the marquee of Steel Pier on WFPG, and from the runway during the Pageant at Convention Hall. Marie had established the famed "She-Shell Award", presented annually to the city's "Outstanding Woman of the Year." The 1984 Easter Parade on our Boardwalk was dedicated to Marie's memory by then-Mayor Michael Matthews.

Wicker rolling chairs made a surprise comeback on our boardwalk in 1984. A Margate man, Larry Belfer saw the potential in these colorful relics of the past and stored almost a hundred of the classy vehicles inside the dark and musty recesses of the Apollo Theatre. Shill had ceased operations a decade earlier, soon after the trams began running. At one time, between 1900 and 1935, Atlantic City had more than 3500 rolling chairs on the wooden way. Now, in 1985, more and more people are discovering, or rediscovering the joys of a ride in a rolling chair.

Prices of new cars continued to escalate with the new Chrysler "Fifth Avenue" going for $13,750 and the Dodge "Aries" for $7,230. Bert

71031 STEEPLECHASE AND BOARDWALK, ATLANTIC CITY, N. J.

and Ralph Saber of B & E Productions presented their 10th Annual Antique and Classic Car Auction and Flea Market at Convention Hall in February with more than 600 vehicles going over the block. When the show began in 1975, fewer than 100 cars were auctioned off. The 3-day show this year attracted more than 60,000 persons. Atlantic City Police Inspector Neil Kane drafted a proposal for a 4-day work week for the department, saying it would eliminate $250,000 in overtime pay for so-called "muster" time. Each person would work a 10-hour day four days a week.

The January "win" at the city's 9 casinos was $131,000,000 with Resorts International, Caesar's and Bally's Park Place finishing in that order. Much expansion was in progress or had been proposed by the gaming halls, with the Sands, formerly the Brighton planning a $26,000,000 addition of an entire top floor of suites exclusively for high-rollers. Among the big names booked into casino showrooms that year were Susan Somers, Buddy Greco and Billy Crystal at the Sands; Tony Bennett, Keely Smith, Allen & Rossi, and Buddy Rich at the Playboy; Joey Travolta at the Claridge; Lou Rawls, Loretta Lynn, and Eddy Arnold at Harrah's; Charlie Callas at Caesar's; Liberace, Joan Rivers, Johnny Mathis, and Tony Orlando at Resorts International; and the sparkling revue "Board-walk Follies" at the Golden Nugget. And the great Italian tenor, Luciano Pavarotti, sang to a packed house outdoors in a huge tent set up by Resorts in March.

The Atlantic City Art Center on Garden Pier had an outstanding display of fine art from the State of Israel featuring 100 works by 30 Israeli artists and craftspersons. Center Director Florence Valore Miller said more and more people were visiting the Center to enjoy the exhibits which are changed quite often. The facility has made a great comeback following a disastrous fire a few years ago.

Atlantic City was becoming, more and more a most popular destination for tourists, and in one month . . . January 1984 . . . nearly 90,000 passengers used the city's two airports, an increase of more than 30% over 1983. Before he lost the recall election, Mayor Matthews came out in support of a takeover of both airports by a county Authority, "so long," he said, "as the city is well-paid, otherwise, forget it." County Sheriff Mario Floriani, a former Atlantic City Police Chief was said to be considering an offer to become Public Safety Director, but it has not happened.

Our beautiful old Seaside Hotel was demolished by its new owners, Resorts International. Built in 1862, the hotel was moved three years later to its Boardwalk at Pennsylvania Avenue site. For a short time in the early 'Twenties, the Seaside was the home of WHAR, Atlantic City's first radio station which operated solely on storage batteries. One of its first engineers, Frank Samaha, now in his late eighties, resides in Atlantic City. The call letters are said to have stood for We Have A Radio. Daily broadcasts by the Seaside Trio were eagerly awaited by audiences of WHAR and WPG. Two good friends of mine, Mildred Fox and the late Hille Rattay were employed by the Seaside for a number of years. Miss Rattay was the daughter of the talented WPG air personality and Public Relations Director Ethel Rattay. And many readers may recall, as I do, enjoyable times spent in the Ruby Room and the Surf 'n' Sand Room of the Seaside.

The number of passengers arriving by casino bus again shot up by almost 2,000,000. The number of buses increased too, with a record 384,358 of them, up by more than 40,000 from 1983. After a two-year period during which no new hotel casino properties were built, the beautiful Trump Plaza opened on the Boardwalk near Convention Hall on May 14. It was our 10th gaming hall.

Another well-known resort personage left the scene in 1984. Paul A. D'Amato, known to just about everyone as "Skinny," passed away following a long illness. D'Amato operated the famous 500 Club, 6 South Missouri Avenue, for years and was responsible for bringing hundreds of big stars to town. He booked his good buddy, Frank Sinatra, into the "5", as it was referred to by the in-crowd, time and again. Maybe you were among the loyal Sinatra fans who stood patiently in lines which snaked around the corner and up the street waiting to see and hear "The Voice". When the club burned to the ground in June, 1973, Skinny D'Amato took the loss very hard and friends say he was never the same after that.

Two local restaurants were torn down in 1984; Shumsky's on Pacific Avenue in Atlantic City and Zaberer's, on the Black Horse Pike, McKee City. Shumsky's was famous for its outstanding Jewish cuisine and had been in the same family for years. Charlie and Rita Zaberer had started on a shoestring with the Gables Inn to go on to phenomenal success. In the early 'eighties, things changed, business dropped off and it was closed. The slogan of the popular Mainland restaurant was "Just Minutes Away" and those words are chiseled on the headstone of Charlie Zaberer in Holy Cross Cemetery, Mays Landing, NJ.

On May 20th, I had the pleasure of being among hundreds of well-wishers and fans who came to the famous Club Harlem for a big bash honoring the one and only Chris Columbo. Looking at this fine gentleman, a talented musician whom I've known for more than 30 years, it was hard to realize he was 82 years old. Chris acts, moves, and thinks like a much younger man and remains active on the entertainment scene. A drummer by profession, "Crazy Chris" as he is lovingly known by his intimates, enjoys nothing more than sitting at his beloved drums and laying down a solid beat. Chris had his own band for years and also traveled all over the nation with Louis Jordan and his Tympany Five. During the swing era, he played the legendary Savoy Ballroom in New York City, "The Home of Happy Feet." In the '50s, Chris became the first black disc jockey on Atlantic City airwaves at WFPG with a record program called the "Swingship" which he co-hosted with his wife, Jessie Morris, herself an accomplished performer as a singer and dancer. Chris, who serves as Vice-President of the Atlantic City Musicians Association, has been a real inspiration to countless musicians over the years and dotes on helping young people to make it in their chosen profession. And oh yes, Chris always says, "Live music is best!"

1985

Atlantic City now has its 11th hotel casino after what was built as the Hilton opened as Trump's Castle in June. The license application by Hilton was turned down and Donald Trump lost no time in purchasing the facility for $300,000,000. The Castle is close by Harrah's Marina Hotel Casino, making it the second gaming hall in that part of town, away from the Boardwalk.

Trump's Castle offers something different in the way of music. George Hernandez, its Musical Director leads a fine Latin-American orchestra, reminding us of the days when just about every Boardwalk hotel featured that type of music. During the forties and fifties, bands led by Tito Puente, Esy Morales, Jose Corbello, Pupi Campo, and Irving Fields played at prime locations. I did the announcing on ABC for Fields "from the beautiful Sun 'n' Star Roof of the Senator Hotel, overlooking downtown Atlantic City" in the 1950s. Then there were the orchestras of Jose Melis, Bobby Roberts, Argueso, Noro Morales, Jose Pillado and the popular accordion-playing leader, Pedro Albani, featured for many seasons at such beach front hotels as the President, Ambassador, Traymore, Mayflower, and Chelsea. Albani continues active on the local entertainment scene, playing for many functions.

Speaking of the Hotel Chelsea which was built soon after 1900, it was renamed the Deauville-Sheraton after it was taken over by that chain in 1962. However, the old Chelsea is no more, having been knocked down by the wrecker's ball in May. On the site, Tropicana plans a huge theme park. And another old hotel, the Holmhurst, 24 S. Pennsylvania Avenue was torn down by its new owners, Resorts International last Spring. The Holmhurst had been owned by the Stitzer family since the mid-30s. And the Shelburne, once one of Atlantic City's premier hotels, on the Boardwalk at Michigan Avenue, is gone too, a victim of progress. It dated back to 1865 and had played host to such luminaries as Diamond Jim Brady and Lillian Russell when she was the toast of the entertainment world. The Morton, on S. Virginia Avenue, near Steel Pier? That's gone too, after being heavily damaged by fire.

Resorts International, always at the forefront in making news, just about floored the city's Fine Arts Commission when it painted its red brick building WHITE! And Resorts' pink blimp has become a familiar sight in the skies over Atlantic City. Incidentally, have you noticed that the initials of the firm spell out R.I.C.H.?

Atlantic City has been famous for unusual publicity stunts since it was founded in 1854, and many world's records have been established here. In June, Fralinger's Original Salt Water Taffy marked its 100th anniversary with a spectacular taffy-pull right in the middle of . . . where else . . . the Boardwalk, and in front of Convention Hall yet! I had the honor of serving as M.C. of the event when more than 250 persons, young and old, took part in producing what has to be the longest piece of salt water taffy ever: 500 feet, 10 inches! It will go into the Guiness Book of World Records. Fralinger's, the oldest original business on the Boardwalk, continues today under the ownership-management of Arthur H. Gager, 3rd, the fourth generation of an unbroken family line to operate the business. The founder was his great-great-great uncle.

Our new Free Public Library was dedicated in August after moving to the new building at Tennessee and Atlantic Avenues. The future of the old Carnegie Library building is undecided. Let's hope it is not torn down, but preserved for its historical value and beauty. There was good news for lovers of the "old" Atlantic City when the dreams of the city's leader in the movement to preserve irreplaceable artifacts, Fine Arts Commission

Chairman Florence Valore Miller came true with the dedication of the Atlantic City Historical Museum on Garden Pier, Sunday, April 14th. Anthony Kutschera is its President. The museum contains such local memorabilia as photographs, silverware, post cards, magazines, glassware, furniture, fixtures, books, advertising matter and more. Admission is free.

A man known to visitors and locals as "Cooks Books," the Singing Cabbie, was found murdered in his cab along the White Horse Pike in Absecon on Palm Sunday. His given name was Raoul Suarez, but he was best known by his unusual nickname which appeared on the doors of his well-kept taxi. I'd often see "Cooks" as I arrived in the city before dawn to go on the air, as he cruised the streets looking for fares. He always had a smile and if he could do you a favor, he would, no questions asked. He hosted a weekly radio show and was on local television for years. His motto could very well apply to all of us: "Every Day is a Miracle." Rest in peace, Cooks.

The Casino Reinvestment Development Authority is now at work, with former Atlantic Electric Chief Executive John Feehan as Chairman. Others on the panel are Mayor James Usry, Irene Smith, Don Thomas, Walter Reade, David Kotok, and merchant-entrepreneur-lecturer and world traveler, Murray Raphel. Their job: to administer the expenditure of more than one and a half billion dollars, $750,000,000 of which is earmarked for Atlantic City alone, mostly for housing. The Rescue Mission on Bacharach Boulevard is looking forward to moving to new quarters in the old warehouse near the bus terminal on Arkansas Avenue. Its Director, Reverend Rex Whiteman says it is serving thousands at its current location and is taxed far beyond capacity. The Atlantic County United Way moved from its old building at 1125 Pacific Avenue this Spring to the Guarantee Building at 1125 Atlantic Avenue. Its Executive Director for more than 30 years, Allan Angelo is now retired, and the new Director is Raymond Jacoby who came down from Burlington, Vermont.

A 12-acre tract Westbound on Route 322, Albany Avenue Boulevard, accommodating 400 casino buses, opened in September. Ole Hansen and Sons, developers of the $2,000,000 facility say it will help alleviate traffic problems created by the more than 900 buses per day coming into Atlantic City. Another lot, built up from meadowland, has opened on Route 30, White Horse Pike Eastbound, near the drawbridge, for employees of Trump's Castle only and they are transported by shuttle to their work.

Earlier in this book, you read about Olivet Presbyterian Church's being converted into a nightclub called Littlejohn's. Well, the club didn't make it and has been torn down. And so has another old church, St. James Episcopal.

Gary Collins marks his 4th year as M.C. of the Miss America Pageant, having replaced Bert Parks' replacement, Ron Ely, in 1982. There is talk that the Pageant finals may be moved to a night other than Saturday to improve TV ratings. If so, another pageant tradition will be lost. For years, Pageant Week began the day after Labor Day, but was moved back a week in 1984. By the time you read this, you'll know that the hauntingly-beautiful song "There She Is, Miss America" by Bernie Wayne, has been reinstated at the Pageant after an absence of four years. It was first used in 1955, when it was sung by emcee Bert Parks.

A massive renovation job on the interior of Convention Hall is nearing completion. The cost: $23,000,000. When the big hall was built in the late 1920s, the entire facility came in at only $15,000,000. The old Hall may be getting a new "sister" if plans materialize for a new Convention Center at the end of the Expressway. The manager of our present Convention Hall is Howard Persina. In early September, we learned that Trump Plaza Hotel Casino . . . the building alone . . . is worth more than Atlantic City's total real estate value in 1977, the year before the first casino opened! As of May, 1985, 155,891 casino charter buses had transported 4,656,590 passengers into town. Employment in the casino industry now stands at approximately 40,000. Total salaries for 1984 were $708,000,000 including fringe benefits and payroll expenses.

With 11 casinos, Atlantic City now has 83 restaurants and "eateries" it did not have 7 years ago. Some hotels have as many as nine dining places, while others have as few as 5. Among all our hotel casinos, there is a total of 1160 table games, 15,928 slot machines, 19,159 parking spaces and more than 6000 hotel rooms. Two more casinos, now building, should open within two years. They are "Showboat" and "Resorts II", both on the city's Urban Renewal Tract.

Well, what do YOU think? Have things moved too quickly during the seven years of gaming? What would have happened had we not gotten approval for gambling? Many hail the industry for creating so much employment; others say it has changed the city too much, too soon, and hurt too many people. Who will be proved right and will it all work out eventually, with Atlantic City regaining its reputation as a family resort, and not merely a mecca for gamblers?

Tune in tomorrow!

Viewing the Miss America pageant parade on the boardwalk.

414:—Steeplechase Pier, Atlantic City, N. J.

Steeplechase Pier

The Peanut Store on the Boardwalk

Sept. 14, 1944, the day after the hurricane, in front of England General and Convalescent Hospital. (From official Army photos)

Hackney's world-famous seafood restaurant is a block long.

Inlet Pier where fishing boats, sailboats, and charter boats are available.

Ladies Parlor, Hotel Dennis

Globe Theatre

View of the spacious Marine Ball Room—Ocean end of Atlantic City Steel Pier

During World War II, more than 60 Atlantic City hotels were taken over by the military "for the duration" for training purposes. Chalfonte-Haddon Hall, now Resorts International Hotel Casino, became England General Hospital where thousands of armed forces personnel were brought for treatment and recuperation. The first Atlantic City man to arrive at England General was U.S. Army Infantry Sergeant James Masland who had been wounded in the North Africa Campaign. (Photo courtesy Mrs. Ernest Harffey)

Kuehnle's Hotel

Atlantic City Casino

Printed sources of information for "Atlantic City Diary".

Atlantic City Casino Association; New Jersey Casino Control Commission

Atlantic City Press

Atlantic City Evening Union

Atlantic City Reporter

Atlantic City Tribune

Boardwalk Illustrated News

"Steel Pier Parade" Magazine

Atlantic City Review

M. E. Blatt Company Diary for 1927

"Book of the Boardwalk" by Frank Butler

"Firefighting By The Seashore" by Franklin Kemp

"So Young, So Gay" by William McMahon

"Atlantic City Illustrated" Magazine

Souvenir program from Warner Theatre opening

"Amusements", various issues, published by Brooks & Idler

ASCAP Hit Songs (Published by American Society of Composers, Authors and Publishers, New York)

B.M.I. Pop Hits (Published by Broadcast Music Inc., New York)

Philadelphia Public Ledger

Atlantic City Gazette Review

Atlantic City Public Library

"Atlantic City and County", published by Albert M. Slocum Company, Philadelpia, Pa., 1899.